Also by Marvin E. Frankel

Criminal Sentences: Law without Order

THE GRAND JURY

The Grand Jury

An Institution on Trial

Marvin E. Frankel
and Gary P. Naftalis

A NEW LEADER BOOK

HILL AND WANG NEW YORK
A division of Farrar, Straus and Giroux

Copyright © 1975, 1977 by
American Labor Conference on International Affairs, Inc.
All rights reserved
Published simultaneously in Canada
by McGraw-Hill Ryerson Ltd., Toronto
Printed in the United States of America
First printing, 1977

Library of Congress Cataloging in Publication Data

Frankel, Marvin E.
  The grand jury.

  "A New leader book."
  Includes bibliographical references and index.
  1. Grand jury—United States. I. Naftalis, Gary P.,
joint author. II. Title.
  KF9642.F7   345'.73'072   77-5459

This book is a revised and expanded version of a special issue
of *The New Leader*. Conceived by the editors of the magazine,
it was produced under a grant from the Tamiment Institute.
It is the first in a series sponsored by the foundation that will
deal with a variety of subjects related to matters of social
welfare.

Contents

THE GRAND JURY

Introduction

Though best known for other clauses, the Fifth Amendment to our federal Constitution provides as its first guarantee the protection of the grand jury. It says: "No person shall be held to answer for a capital, or otherwise infamous crime, unless on a presentment or indictment of a Grand Jury, except in cases arising in the land or naval forces, or in the Militia, when in actual service in time of War or public danger. . . ." This meant, and on the federal level still means, that a person may not be brought to trial for a serious crime (generally a felony—an offense punishable by over a year in prison) unless a grand jury has heard enough evidence to return an indictment.

Transplanted from England, the grand jury was seen by the Founders as a bulwark for the individual against arbitrary or malevolent prosecutors. It was also valued as a kind of people's watchdog, to search out and disclose governmental imperfections, corruption, or matters needing legislative reform. These purposes, so dear to the liberties and the authority of the people, entitled the grand jury to be enshrined in the Bill of Rights.

Frequently referred to as the People's Panel, the grand jury certainly was something else when it was born about eight hundred years ago. In fact, it was the King's Panel, commissioned to investigate for the monarch, enforce his writ, extend and help consolidate his power. After centuries of sometimes accidental evolution, the institution developed into, and pretty much remains, the Prosecutor's Panel, largely directed and controlled by the government lawyers—elected or appointed—charged with enforcing the criminal laws and prosecuting alleged violators.

It may be that the grand jury never was, never became, and never could quite become a People's Panel in any genuine sense. It may be, as many have long asserted, that the inability to realize the ideal should prompt us to abolish the imperfect substitute. But the sensible course would seem to be to inquire first whether the grand jury's imperfections are remediable, whether it might yet serve the high purposes, and assure the high protections, the Founders envisioned.

Whichever path we follow, the issue is surely the people's problem. The grand jury today is a powerful instrument, for good and for ill. As the Supreme Court observed a while ago, reiterating a point it had made in 1919:

> Traditionally the grand jury has been accorded wide latitude to inquire into violations of criminal law. No judge presides to monitor its proceedings. It deliberates in secret and may determine alone the course of its inquiry. The grand jury may compel the production of evidence or the testimony of witnesses as it considers appropriate, and its operation generally is unrestrained by the technical

procedural and evidentiary rules governing the conduct of criminal trials. "It is a grand inquest, a body with powers of investigation and inquisition, the scope of whose inquiries is not to be limited narrowly by questions of propriety or forecasts of the probable result of the investigation, or by doubts whether any particular individual will be found properly subject to an accusation of crime." *Blair v. United States,* 250 U.S. 273, 282 . . . (1919).[1]

Given its awesome range of powers, the grand jury clearly demands attentive understanding. In the pages that follow we try to meet the demand by starting with an examination of the grand jury's history, its various manifestations, its functions and practices. Against this account of its actual operation and doctrinal foundations, we then take up the main problems and conflicts that have for so long made the grand jury a subject of controversy. Finally, we outline the major proposals for federal reform now pending in the Congress, and we present our own views on some debatable questions.

1

Origins
and Development

The ancestor of the grand jury is said by historians to date from 1166, the year of King Henry II's Assize of Clarendon. The idea of the Grand Assize (as it was known in Norman French) was to employ a body of knowledgeable local gentry as the king's investigative arm.

The infant grand jury, like most institutions that survive to grow old, was far different from what it has become. Drawn from the rural neighborhood in which they sat, the grand jurors themselves were primary sources of "evidence," reporting and acting on things they knew firsthand or had heard, including rumors and gossip. Today, in the swirling anonymities of the great cities where grand juries mostly sit, it would be the rare (and, indeed, somewhat questionable) case where a grand juror acted on anything within his or her personal ken, rather than upon knowledge acquired for the first time from testimony and exhibits "presented" by a government lawyer in the grand jury room.

Another difference was the relative subservience of the

original grand jury to the king and his judges. Henry II, in promulgating the Assize of Clarendon, was not in the least concerned with creating a shield for the citizen in his dealings with the state. The Grand Assize was established to enable the king to wrest the administration of justice from the Church and the feudal barons. The grand jury would be primarily a weapon for the monarch —enforcing his law, whether or not that could aptly be called at any given time the "king's peace."

Not only did the grand jury seven to eight hundred years ago fail to protect the subject; its accusing voice was far closer to condemnation than the contemporary indictment. In today's legal theory, an indicted defendant is "presumed to be innocent" and receives his "day in court" before a separate trial jury. Not so in medieval times. Accusation by the Grand Assize was followed by "trial" in the form of ordeal, a harrowing process offering slender chance of vindication. A historian has provided this description of the four species of ordeal—cold water, hot water, hot iron, and morsel:

Each was undergone after the most solemn religious ceremonial. In the case of the cold-water ordeal, a fast of three days' duration was first submitted to in the presence of a priest; then the accused was brought into the church, where mass was chanted, followed by the communion. Before communion, however, the accused was adjured by the Father, Son and Holy Ghost, by the Christian religion which he professed, by the only-begotten Son, by the Holy Trinity, by the Holy Gospels, and by the holy relics, not to partake of the communion if he was guilty. Prayers, reading of the Scriptures, intercessions and benedictions followed. Communion having been partaken, *adjuratio aquae* was made by the priest; in which the water was asked to cast forth the accused if guilty, and to receive him into its depths if innocent. After these ceremonies, the accused was stripped, kissed the book and the cross, was sprinkled with holy water, and then cast into the depths. If he sank, he was adjudged not guilty; if he swam, he was pronounced guilty.

Similar religious ceremonies were performed in the other forms of ordeal. If the accuser elected for the accused the trial by hot water, the water was placed in a vessel and heated to the highest degree. Then, if the party were accused of an inferior crime, he plunged his arm into the water as far as the wrist, and brought forth a stone suspended by a cord; if he were accused of a great crime, the stone was suspended deeper, so as to require him to plunge his arm into the water as far as his elbow. The hand of the accused was then bandaged, and at the end of three days the bandage was removed. If it now appeared that the wound had healed, the accused was deemed innocent; but if it had festered, he was held guilty.

If trial by hot iron was elected, a piece of iron weighing either one or three pounds, according to the nature of the crime charged, was heated under the direction of men standing by, whose duty it was to see that a proper heat was obtained and kept until the time for the test had nearly arrived. During the final ceremonies the fire was left, and the iron allowed to remain in the embers. It was then raised, and, with an invocation to the Deity, given into the naked hand of the accused, who carried it the distance of nine feet, when it was dropped, and the hand bandaged as in the case of the hot water ordeal, to abide the same test.

The ordeal of the morsel, accompanied by similar ceremonials, was undergone by the accused undertaking to swallow a piece of barley bread, or a piece of cheese, of the weight of an ounce . . . if he succeeded without serious difficulty, he was deemed innocent, but if he choked and grew black in the face, he was adjudged guilty.[2]

Since the topic is the grand jury, not trial procedure, we resist the lure of much more history between the ordeal and contemporary trial practice. Suffice it to say, first, that the ideal of a rational means for truth seeking in court remains to be achieved; and, second, that the grand jury, like the interrelated procedures for trial, evolved and changed over the centuries. In 1215, for example, the Lateran Council abolished trial by ordeal, and the defendant was then tried by the very same jury that had indicted him. Obviously, a defendant did not have bright prospects of prevailing before the panel that had accused him. Nor were his chances improved by the power and practice of the royal judges to fine and imprison jurors who found a defendant not guilty.

Continuing the slow course of progress, by the middle of the fourteenth century English procedures reached the point where the accused could strike from the trial jury any member of the grand jury that had indicted him. About the same time, the grand jury began to hear testimony in private, a practice that gave rise to grand jury secrecy, which remains a fundamental concept today.

But the notion of the grand jury as a protector against unfounded charges and oppressive government was a long time in coming. It was not until 1681, some five hundred years after the Assize of Clarendon, that this function made its first significant appearance in the cases of Anthony, Earl of Shaftesbury, and Stephen Colledge.

The two men were vocal Protestant opponents of King Charles II's attempt to re-establish the Catholic Church in England. The king and his royal prosecutors sought to have them indicted for treason and demanded that the grand jury proceeding be held in public. The panel resisted, exercising its power to question the witnesses in private without the presence of the royal prosecutors, and after hearing the evidence refused to indict. The Colledge and Shaftesbury cases have been generally hailed as marking the grand jury's initial assertion of its role as a shield for the innocent against malicious and oppressive prosecution.

The development can be traced to several factors. To

begin with, the hearing of witnesses in private enabled the panel to withstand pressure from the crown and its representatives. In addition, the failure of trial juries to protect the accused because the crown was empowered to fine and imprison jurors who had the temerity to say "not guilty" left a vacuum to be filled. Finally, the new role of the grand jury was enhanced by the discontinuance of the practice of judges cross-examining grand jurors about their findings.

Incidentally, despite the landmark nature of their cases, events did not end happily for Shaftesbury and Colledge. Undaunted by the grand jury's refusal to indict Colledge, the king had the case presented again to a different grand jury in the more friendly town of Oxford; it returned a true bill, and Colledge was convicted and executed. Shaftesbury fled to Holland, where he remained in exile for the brief period until his death in 1683.

The English colonists, meanwhile, not only brought their language to the new world; they brought their institutions. The grand juries, besides serving as the initiators of prosecutions, acted in several of the colonies as spokesmen for the people, sounding boards for their leaders, and vehicles for complaints against officialdom.

Grand jurors in the colonies inspected and reported on the condition of public roads, the performance of public officials, and the expenditure of public funds. In New York, the grand jury successfully petitioned the Duke of York to grant the colony an elected assembly. Subsequently, the crown abolished this newly created assembly and the grand jury expanded its powers accordingly. Colonial New York grand juries engaged in such legislative functions as ordering dispensers of alcoholic beverages to provide lodging for their patrons.

In Boston, grand juries mobilized public opinion behind movements for improved public administration.

When a grand jury threatened to indict the city of Boston for not keeping the streets in safe condition, the Town Meeting reacted by repairing the streets rather than hiring a lawyer to defend it in a criminal prosecution. In Annapolis, grand jury protests against corruption and incompetence forced the city council to meet regularly and to be more responsive to the people's needs.

As in the mother country, colonial grand juries undertook to protect the individual from oppression. The most celebrated instance, although by no means the only one, was the 1743 case of John Peter Zenger. A New York newspaper publisher, Zenger had criticized the colony's governor, who sought to have him prosecuted for criminal libel. Two grand juries refused to indict. The royal authorities then prosecuted him by information—a written accusation drawn up by a prosecutor—but the trial jury refused to convict. Zenger's name is remembered today mainly for his role in the struggle for free expression. The glory is sufficient, however, for sharing with his anonymous fellow citizens on the grand and trial juries.

When relations between the American colonies and Great Britain grew increasingly tense, grand juries became a means of protesting abuses by the crown's emissaries. In 1765, a Boston panel refused to indict those who had led riots against the Stamp Act. Four years later, a Boston grand jury indicted British soldiers quartered in the town for offenses against the populace, while at the same time refusing to indict persons charged by the royal authorities with inciting these soldiers to desert. In Philadelphia, a grand jury initiated a program of resistance to British rule; it denounced the use of the tea tax to pay the salaries of British officials, promoted a boycott of British goods, and called for collective action with the other colonies for redress of grievances.

The broad sweep of grand jury activities continued

through the Revolution. The panels functioned as both patriotic organs and propaganda agencies, adopting resolutions condemning Great Britain and urging the people to support the struggle for freedom. In some instances, the calls to arms were sounded by the grand jurors themselves; in others, the sparks came from patriotic oratory by the presiding judges in their charges to the grand jury. These judicial incitements bore no relation to the relatively private charges of judges to grand juries that are customary today; they were given wide circulation by the press and added fuel to the revolutionary fire.

Like any agency of government, the grand jury throughout its history has reflected the character and the tensions of its political environment. Thus, in the early years of the United States, with the Fifth Amendment and the grand jury emplaced in the Constitution, the bitter struggles between the Federalists (George Washington, John Adams, Alexander Hamilton, and company) and Thomas Jefferson's Republicans erupted regularly during grand jury proceedings.

Federalist judges, the law-and-order people of their time, lectured grand jurors on the need for vigorous enforcement of Federalist statutes, including the ill-famed Alien and Sedition Acts. The Sedition Act of 1789 made it a crime, punishable by a $5,000 fine and five years in prison, "if any person shall write, print, utter or publish . . . any false, scandalous and malicious writing or writings against the government of the United States or either house of Congress . . . or the President . . . with intent to defame . . . or to bring them, or either of them, into contempt or disrepute; or to excite against them, or either of them, the hatred of the good people of the United States."

Almost two hundred years later, in 1964, the Supreme

Court mentioned that the quoted law had been an unconstitutional invasion of the right of free expression protected by the First Amendment.[3] In its time, though, it served to repress and punish many opponents of the Federalist Administration. Federalist judges took leadership roles in pressing grand juries to indict Republican spokesmen, especially newspaper publishers who were critical of the government. This partisan use of grand juries did not stop with the indictment of Republican critics. Federalist judges went so far as to harangue grand juries on the need to elect John Adams President in 1800, concurrently denouncing Jefferson and branding his supporters as radicals and malcontents.

With the Federalists controlling the judiciary, Republican responses were not much heard in the federal courts. But Jeffersonian judges on state benches were vocal in opposition. They spoke out on the evils of the Alien and Sedition laws and emphasized the importance of the grand jury as a barrier against unjust prosecutions.

The embroilment of grand juries in politics did not end with Jefferson's election as President in 1800. In the most famous incident of the Republican chapter, Jefferson's Administration sought to have his political enemy Aaron Burr prosecuted for treason. As in the Shaftesbury and Colledge cases, the grand jury refused to indict. The case was re-presented to a specially selected grand jury in Jefferson's native Virginia and Burr was indicted. But he was eventually acquitted, and students have continued to question whether there was sufficient evidence to justify the prosecution in the first place.

Similar examples of political divisions affecting grand jury proceedings were to appear shortly before and during the Civil War. In the antebellum period, grand juries in the South, acting vigorously to uphold the practice of slavery, returned indictments against abolitionist leaders and newspapers. In the North, grand juries were rarely concerned with the slavery question until 1850, when passage of the Fugitive Slave Law made assisting runaway slaves a criminal offense. After that, the impact of local political sentiment could be seen in the spotty enforcement of the law, persistently denounced by abolitionist leaders and the press.

During the Civil War, grand juries played political roles reminiscent of those adopted in the Revolution. Judges in their charges assailed the enemy and encouraged support of the war. In the North, many judges defined treason very broadly in their addresses to the grand juries; the jurors more often than not responded by indicting pro-Southern citizens and important officials of the Confederacy. Antiwar publications felt the wrath of patriotic grand jurors. In New York City, a grand jury publicly warned three newspapers, including the *New York Daily News* and the *Brooklyn Eagle,* that they were encouraging the rebels. This public criticism was followed by federal action banning these newspapers from the mails because of disloyalty.

During the Reconstruction period, the grand jury served as a principal weapon of Southern whites in their struggle against radical Republicans and Negro rights. The whites gained control of state grand juries, which returned scores of indictments against the so-called scalawags and carpetbaggers. Although many of the indictments were never brought to trial, they were frequently effective in driving carpetbaggers out of the South.

At the same time, Southern white grand juries refused to indict members of the Ku Klux Klan and others who intimidated blacks, and they made no attempt to enforce the laws granting suffrage. The reaction was predictable: federal legislation protecting voting and other civil rights was enacted, and sometimes even enforced by federal grand juries. In a small portent of the civil-rights struggle of the 1960's, state and federal grand juries would occasionally reach different conclusions when dealing with the same facts. Where state panels found nothing amiss, federal grand juries indicted Southern whites for fraud and intimidation.

Long before Watergate, grand juries took the lead in battling political corruption. Often they acted on their own initiative in the face of opposition from a district attorney. In New York City, in 1872, an extensive grand jury probe toppled the notorious Boss Tweed and his cronies. Since the district attorney was closely associated with Tweed, the panel acted independently of him, conducting its own investigation and interviewing witnesses without the prosecutor's help.

In Minneapolis, in 1902, a grand jury hired its own private detectives and amassed evidence sufficient to indict the mayor and cause the chief of police to resign. After removing these officials, the grand jury acted as a committee of public safety and effectively governed the city. Five years later, in San Francisco, a grand jury indicted the mayor and named a new reform mayor to run the city.

Other issues of magnitude—for example, the struggle of Mormon polygamists against the prevailing commitment to monogamy, the conflict between big business and the newly developing labor unions, and the early vendettas of this century against "foreign radicalism"— were echoed in grand jury proceedings. But the grand jury is no longer a forum for hot political and ideological contests. Dramatic, sometimes violent confrontations between grand juries and prosecutors, politicians, legislatures, even within the grand juries themselves, became largely things of the past by about the 1930's.

The one argument that goes on unabated after nearly two hundred years, and that is central for the present discussion, concerns the utility and desirability of the institution itself. Whatever the Founders believed, the grand jury has not been the object of uniform admiration. England, whence it came, abolished it in 1933. In this country there has been a discernible trend toward its non-use. As early as 1859, Michigan became the first state to eliminate the stipulation that criminal prosecutions must be initiated by a grand jury. Other states, particularly those more recently admitted to the Union, have followed Michigan's lead.

The situation as of now is that the grand jury continues for the federal sphere, the Fifth Amendment remaining intact along with the rest of the Bill of Rights. Among the states, twenty-two require a grand jury indictment in felony cases, three require it only when the crime is punishable by death or life imprisonment, and in the other twenty-five a prosecutor launching a criminal case may elect whether to seek an indictment or simply to file an information. As a result, in most of these last jurisdictions the grand jury is resorted to infrequently.

Like most substantial institutions of any age, the grand jury has always had friends and detractors. It has been assailed as inefficient, an obstruction, a pointless rubber stamp for the prosecutor. In recent years, people of libertarian bent have found it an ironic item for inclusion in the Bill of Rights, complaining that it is used to harass the unpopular, to chill free expression, to trap unwary witnesses on contrived perjury charges, and to oppress those summoned to its secret chambers.

On the other side, it is still defended as a safeguard against oppressive prosecutions, although its proponents usually acknowledge its limitations. It is held up, too, as a better tool of investigation than any of the substitutes that might be chosen for this indispensable task.

The rosters of critics and defenders have both been studded with illustrious names over the years. Among the numerous opponents in England were Jeremy Bentham and Robert Peel. The supporters, finally defeated, were less numerous but could boast the great legal historian W. S. Holdsworth and a few other august traditionalists.

In the United States the enemies of the grand jury have included Roscoe Pound, Justice Felix Frankfurter, Raymond Moley, former President and Chief Justice William Howard Taft, and Wayne Morse (while Dean of the Oregon Law School). Backing the institution have been such notables as Justice Hugo L. Black, Frank Hogan, Estes Kefauver, Thomas E. Dewey, and a number of grand jurors' associations—perhaps the most famous and vocal being the Grand Jury Association of New York County, which, whether this is a portent or not, went out of business in 1971.

All this moves us, of course, toward the central issues of this book: whether the grand jury ought to survive and how it should be employed. But useful answers to these ultimate questions require that we have some serious understanding of what the institution is and does in its current incarnation.

2

Theory
and Practice

With fifty-odd separate jurisdictions, our federal system is a lawyer's dream (or nightmare) of complex varieties. It is impossible to generalize about the number of citizens who constitute a grand jury or the number of grand jurors whose concurrence is necessary for an indictment. Practice differs between federal and state courts, and varies again from state to state.

In the federal courts, the procedure is uniform. The grand jury is a body of twenty-three citizens empowered to operate with a quorum of sixteen, and twelve votes are required to return an indictment. How and why the number twenty-three was settled upon is a short story, mostly because no one is really sure. Holdsworth records that the Grand Assize of 1166 was made up of twelve neighborhood knights. Soon the selection procedure in England became formalized: twenty-four persons from the county were summoned and twenty-three of these were picked for service, with a majority needed to "find a true bill." This practice remained as the common law rule.*

*There is curiosity in, but seemingly no evidence for, the speculation that the

In the states all kinds of numerical combinations and permutations exist, but nowhere does the maximum number of grand jurors exceed twenty-three. In Virginia, as few as five persons constitute a grand jury; in Indiana and South Dakota, only six; and in Oregon, Iowa, Montana, and Utah, seven are sufficient. As for the number of votes needed to return an indictment, some states adhere to the federal rule of twelve; in others the range is anywhere from four to nine. One state, Tennessee, has a unique approach: the grand jury is composed of twelve citizens and the twelve must agree before an indictment may be found.

Irrespective of their numerical composition, all grand juries have a common function: to determine if there is sufficient evidence to warrant putting the subject of an investigation on trial, where the question of guilt or innocence can be determined. In performing this role, the grand jury enjoys extensive powers. Said to have "a right to every man's evidence" (in the absence of some recognized privilege), it is permitted to compel the testimony of witnesses and the production of physical or documentary evidence without observing all the evidentiary and exclusionary rules that apply at trial. It may probe broadly and investigate on the basis of tips, hearsay, and speculation, but there are limits to its investigatory power. Although evidence properly obtained by the grand jury may be used in a civil action subsequently brought by the government, the grand jury must not be used to investigate and gather evidence solely for a civil lawsuit. Similarly, it may not be used solely to obtain evidence against someone who has already been in-

---

number twenty-three is somehow traceable to the ancient Jewish twenty-three-member tribunal known as the Sanhedrin K'tanah, or Lesser Sanhedrin, which served for a number of centuries as an ecclesiastical and secular court until the destruction of the Second Temple in A.D. 70.

dicted. This last rule is sometimes evaded by prosecutors who are less than scrupulous; nevertheless, it is settled law and violations may result in suppression of evidence, among other sanctions.

Formally and technically—albeit in substance only somewhat—the grand jury is an arm and creature of the court. This is most apparent when its powers are questioned or resisted. Then, before the force of the government may be duly exerted, it is necessary to go to a judge for a ruling.

A common situation is that of the person summoned by a grand jury who refuses to turn up, or, having appeared, refuses to cooperate. He cannot be compelled to testify or be punished for not doing so until a judge enters an order commanding compliance. While most applications for such orders are granted, this is a point where the grand jury's powers are tested. If it is found, for example, that the grand jury is seeking to violate a privilege of the witness or to pursue leads obtained by illegal electronic surveillance, the balking witness will be sustained.

But the overwhelming majority of witnesses comply without much trouble, for in reality they have few legal defenses. A witness in most jurisdictions may not refuse to answer questions because he feels they are irrelevant to an inquiry, since the grand jury is permitted to rove widely and (at least on the federal level) need not specify precisely what it is pursuing. (In New York State, and probably elsewhere, a witness may refuse to answer irrelevant questions at the risk of punishment for contempt if a court disagrees with his views on relevance.) A witness may remain silent and rely on his Fifth Amendment privilege against self-incrimination, but that may be overridden by a grant of immunity.

Grand jury subpoenas requiring the production of documents are, as a practical matter, no less difficult to resist. A witness opposing a subpoena must (unless there is some applicable privilege) establish that the documents being sought "can have no conceivable relevance to any legitimate object of investigation by the federal grand jury"[4]—a burden of persuasion that is difficult to understand exactly, let alone sustain to a court's satisfaction.

Nor does a witness have much hope of prevailing when he complains, as many do, that a subpoena is unduly broad or burdensome. In a celebrated case, the court upheld a subpoena for a company's records covering a twenty-year period, despite the fact that merely gathering the materials to meet an earlier subpoena, covering ten years, had kept twenty-six men at work for two months.[5] Moreover, it is expensive, and it may be (or seem) unwise to fight the grand jury.

Most of those summoned find it prudent and expedient to respond to questions, although at times, especially when business organizations are interrogated, the process is likely to be one of negotiation and not collision. Questions may be rephrased or limited in scope. A subpoena for records covering several years may be satisfied, by agreement, with delivery of the files for a substantially shorter period. Matters of privilege or of the witness's personal convenience may be resolved informally or compromised.

In all this routine business of the investigatory machine, the court is an absentee landlord. The show is run by the prosecutors—the United States attorney and his assistants, the local state attorneys (the DA's, solicitors, etc.), or state attorneys general and their staffs. The prosecutors decide what is to be investigated, who will be brought before the grand jurors, and—practically and generally speaking—who should be indicted for what.

True, the grand jury may refuse to indict, and its decision is unreviewable—except that the prosecutor can present the same evidence to another grand jury and try once more to obtain an indictment. Although there is disagreement over the last procedure, it is still permissible. (In New York State prosecutors are somewhat more restricted; a charge on which a grand jury has refused to indict may be resubmitted only by order of a judge.)

The grand jury also may "run away" and explore on its own, or at least initiate lines of inquiry. It may order the prosecutor to draft an indictment, but cannot compel his signature, an act necessary for an indictment to be valid. Nevertheless, even the President of the United States cannot prevent the grand jury from fully investigating a matter and returning an indictment. In one celebrated case, the trial court instructed the panel that it was free to ignore the orders of President Hayes to the prosecutor that the grand jury limit its probe: "The moment the Executive is allowed to control the action of the courts in the administration of criminal justice their independence is gone."[6] Still, these are extraordinary situations.

Day in and day out, the grand jury affirms what the prosecutor calls upon it to affirm—investigating as it is led, ignoring what it is never advised to notice, failing to indict or indicting as the prosecutor "submits" that it should. Not surprisingly, the somewhat technical, somewhat complex, occasionally arcane language of indictments is drafted by the prosecutor and handed to the grand jury foreman or forelady for the signature which is almost invariably affixed.

It could not more than rarely be otherwise. In a busy, densely populated, elaborately organized society— where crime is rife, criminals are tough, many wrongs are mysterious and concealed from laymen—law enforcement is inescapably for professionals. The very notion of the grand jury as beneficent for a free society would be subverted by a band of amateurs engaged in sleuthing, summoning, indicting, or not indicting as their "independent" and untutored judgment might dictate. Privacy, security, and reputation would be in steady jeopardy. Sophisticated criminals would be safe; innocent citizens would be less safe.

So it is not profitable to mourn the grand jury's "loss" of independence. An independent grand jury would be intolerable. The meaningful issues relate to the nature and character of the prosecutorial leadership, the presence or absence of safeguards and countervailing powers, and the nature of the authority formally invested in the grand jury. It is also important that grand juries be adequately educated and sensitized to their powers to ask questions, to be enlightened, to instigate on occasion, and to say no. These are among our major concerns, and will be taken up in detail later. For the moment, let us tarry a while longer over the daily operation of the institution.

The regular work of the ordinary grand jury is secret and unnoticed. Secrecy is a dark notion with Americans, usually for splendid reasons. But the secrecy of the grand jury is basically a good idea, as abused and perverted as it often is. The elementary reasons for it were summarized this way by the Supreme Court:

(1) To prevent the escape of those whose indictment may be contemplated; (2) to insure the utmost freedom to the grand jury in its deliberations, and to prevent persons subject to indictment or their friends from importuning the grand jurors; (3) to prevent subornation of perjury or tampering with the witnesses who may testify before [the] grand jury and later appear at the trial of those indicted by it; (4) to encourage free and untrammeled disclosures by persons

who have information with respect to the commission of crimes; (5) to protect [the] innocent accused who is exonerated from disclosure of the fact that he has been under investigation, and from the expense of standing trial where there was no probability of guilt.[7]

In contemporary experience, the effort to enforce secrecy is too frequently defeated by "leaks." And where a defendant wishes (after indictment, naturally) to see what went on before the grand jury, the claims for secrecy have tended to be pushed by prosecutors beyond the fair limits of their logic.

With regard to counsel, generally the witness is prohibited from having his lawyer accompany him when he testifies before the grand jury; only a handful of states allow the presence of counsel in the grand jury room. But there is, as we shall see, considerable pressure to extend this practice.

Although the matter of fair grand jury procedure is vital, the immediate issue is whether a person under investigation should be indicted. The standard for determining this is easily stated in two questions: (1) Has a crime been committed? (2) Is there "probable cause" to believe the person being investigated did it? Yet, like other criteria for what we call "weighing" evidence, the notion of probable cause is not reducible to mechanical tests. In each case it is necessary to decide if the evidence seems sufficient to put the accused through the misery of an indictment and a defense. This, in turn, triggers a host of additional questions that occupy the legal profession and produce disparate answers from the courts.

For example, should an indicted person, given the trauma of indictment itself, be entitled to defeat the prosecution by showing that the evidence presented to the grand jury was not sufficient to indict? Some state courts answer this pretty much in the affirmative (the phrase "pretty much" identifying limits more refined than we need to deal with here). That means fairly ready access to the grand jury's minutes, where they exist, to test the sufficiency of the evidence.

The federal courts and other states take an opposite view. Once indicted, these courts hold, a defendant is adequately protected by the requirement of proof beyond a reasonable doubt before a unanimous trial jury may convict. It is not thought right or necessary, either prior to or after a conviction, to run a further trial of the grand jury's decision to indict. Our own inclinations favor this position. Except possibly in egregious cases of grand jury irresponsibility, a trial jury's verdict ought to be test enough of the sufficiency of the evidence.

Living and working in New York, one of the states where the evidence presented to the grand jury may be challenged, we have heard and read about a fair number of cases in which a state grand jury indictment issued on patently inadequate evidence was dismissed without trial after a judge merely read the grand jury's flimsy record. It is difficult to determine whether such rulings usually end the cases or tend more often to result in new, less vulnerable indictments after more careful presentations to the grand jury. Should it become a common occurrence for prosecutors carelessly, or deliberately, to invite grand jurors to indict on evidence clearly insufficient, pretrial review of the grand jury transcript is a sensible, if not exclusive or indispensable, remedy. From our experience, at present this seems unnecessary. Prosecutors do sometimes worry too much about their batting averages, but indicting without enough evidence is a poor way to swell the rate of convictions. In addition, for the presumably rare prosecutor who harasses a defendant by knowingly procuring an unfounded indictment, the perhaps too infrequently employed disciplinary powers of the court and the bar ought to be wheeled into action.

In short, without urging that it is always the best position, we believe it is generally sound to have only one trial—the one before a petit jury, in open court—to decide the sufficiency of the evidence against an accused person. By and large, we support a comparable approach to questions about rules of evidence being offended in grand jury testimony. Here again there are sharp differences of opinion; issues concerning the "competency" of evidence presented to a grand jury have generated quantities of interesting and divergent decisions.

The Anglo-American rules of evidence, elaborate and finicky beyond any counterparts elsewhere in the world, have evolved mainly to regulate *adversary proceedings before a trial jury.* The procedure of question-and-answer testimony is designed to afford an opportunity for the opposing lawyer to rise up and object that the information to be elicited is forbidden. It may be said to be irrelevant, privileged, unduly prejudicial, or otherwise excludable. It may be hearsay (as where the witness proposes to declare that X told him the defendant shot the victim, without X being present to be cross-examined). There may be other objections. But the heart of the procedure is the objection. Normally, evidence received without objection is not grounds for reversal on appeal.

In the grand jury room there is nobody to object. There is no adversary. The setting is not one where the rules of evidence customarily operate. Is it wrong, then, for the grand jury to consider "incompetent" evidence as a basis for indicting? To answer only briefly, in general the use of some evidence that would have been excluded on objection at a trial is not considered grounds for vitiating an indictment. Where *all* the evidence would be technically inadmissible, the situation is more complicated.

In 1956 the Supreme Court held that an indictment resting wholly on hearsay evidence was valid. The High Court has never qualified that rule, and in the federal courts and in most states indictments may be based solely on hearsay. But there has been a drift toward more limited license. Some lower courts have held, for instance, that where the grand jurors are misled into believing they are getting firsthand testimony rather than hearsay, the deception will cause an indictment to be so defective that a conviction based upon it will be set aside. Consequently, while hearsay may still serve as the basis for an indictment, it has been held that the prosecutor may not mislead the grand jury into thinking that it is receiving better evidence.[8]

Questions have also arisen when the grand jury has used evidence procured by illegal wiretaps or improperly seized in lawless searches. As a rule, a defendant may not successfully complain that an indictment is defective because evidence unconstitutionally obtained or otherwise tainted was presented to the grand jury. His remedy is to have such evidence excluded at trial. The rationale for this was set out in a recent Supreme Court decision. Speaking for the majority, Mr. Justice Lewis F. Powell, Jr., looked to the grand jury's historical role.

> In deciding whether to extend the exclusionary rule to grand jury proceedings, we must weigh the potential injury to the historic role and functions of the grand jury against the potential benefits of the rule as applied in this context. It is evident that this extension of the exclusionary rule would seriously impede the grand jury. Because the grand jury does not finally adjudicate guilt or innocence, it has traditionally been allowed to pursue its investigative and accusatorial functions unimpeded by the evidentiary and procedural restrictions applicable to a criminal trial. Permitting witnesses to invoke the exclusionary rule before a

grand jury would precipitate adjudication of issues hitherto reserved for the trial on the merits and would delay and disrupt grand jury proceedings. Suppression hearings would halt the orderly progress of an investigation and might necessitate extended litigation of issues only tangentially related to the grand jury's primary objective. The probable result would be "protracted interruption of grand jury proceedings," . . . effectively transforming them into preliminary trials on the merits. In some cases, the delay might be fatal to the enforcement of the criminal law.

The opinion concluded: "In sum, we believe that allowing a grand jury witness to invoke the exclusionary rule would unduly interfere with the effective and expeditious discharge of the grand jury's duties."[9]

The grand jury may not force a witness to answer questions or produce records that violate his Fifth Amendment right of silence, however, unless immunity is granted. Nor may the grand jury violate any other valid privilege of the witness. Congress, in Rules of Evidence effective in 1975, designated various privileges applicable in the grand jury room even while providing that most of the rules do not apply there. This has created some uncertainty and will require refinements by the judges. Since, as we have said, the principles of evidence (including various privileges, like those for communications between spouses, between priest and penitent, between lawyer and client, among others) assume an adversary trial, with lawyers ready to object to improper questions, there is a measure of incongruity in saying the rules "apply" in the grand jury room. But it is not wholly meaningless to say this. For one thing, although the witness may not under prevailing practice have his lawyer with him in the grand jury room, he may normally demand leave to consult counsel in an anteroom when there is a claimed need. As a result, it is far from uncommon to have a witness invoke a privilege successfully against a grand jury question.

Furthermore, even though our model is the adversary contest, the courts are not powerless to demand that prosecutors heed the rules and protect the rights of uncounseled people before grand juries. In an interesting opinion late in 1975, Judge Jack B. Weinstein of the Federal District Court in Brooklyn, a noted teacher and expert on the law of evidence, reflected at some length about the uncertain operation of privileges in grand jury interrogation. In the particular case before him, he was asked to overturn a conviction after trial because the grand jury (though not the trial jury thereafter) had heard some evidence said to violate the attorney-client privilege. The claim of privilege was at best a close one, so there was no suggestion that the prosecutor conducting the grand jury proceedings had been slipshod or indifferent to the defendant's rights. For that and a complex of other reasons, the conviction was not set aside.

But Judge Weinstein made it clear that a prosecutor "should not knowingly violate a privilege before the grand jury. He should be sensitive to possible problems. If there is any substantial possibility of a valid claim of privilege he should bring this fact to the attention of the witness, advising the witness of the right to consult counsel; to have the court appoint a lawyer if he cannot afford one; to refuse to answer questions if he believes a privilege may be involved; and to be brought before the court for a ruling."[10] Having said that, the judge noted with approval the apparent policy of the United States attorney in his district "to comply with these guidelines."

Congress has imposed other limits on the kinds of evidence a grand jury may hear, leading to results that seem at least a little anomalous. Under the Omnibus

Crime Control and Safe Streets Act of 1968, evidence obtained by illegal electronic surveillance may not be presented to a grand jury. Thus, a grand jury witness may not be asked questions based upon information obtained as a result of unlawful bugging or wiretapping. But such limitations are narrow and specific: where a statute does not exist, inquiry is permitted. This means that the same grand jury witness may be questioned on the basis of evidence obtained in an illegal search of his car, home, or person, though this violates the Constitution.

Indictments are also generally not subject to attack because the grand jury has not heard all the evidence bearing on a crime. Obviously, the prospective defendant's version of the facts could be highly relevant. Yet, for the most part the subject of investigation has no right to testify before the grand jury unless subpoenaed to appear. Neither does the prospective defendant usually have a right to compel the grand jury to hear witnesses who may testify favorably for his cause, nor is he permitted to be present when the witnesses against him testify. In this regard, the grand jury proceeding differs from a trial, where the accused has a constitutional right to be present and confront his accusers.

Like most things in our multifarious federal system of over fifty legal jurisdictions, however, the last is subject to exceptions and qualifications. Connecticut, in cases punishable by death or life imprisonment, replaces the standard grand jury with a hybrid incorporating some features of the trial process. As described by the United States Court of Appeals for the Second Circuit, the "unique features of the Connecticut grand jury procedure" include:

> (1) Neither the State's Attorney nor any counsel for the prosecution is allowed to appear before the grand jury. The

prosecutor remains outside the grand jury room and sends the State's witnesses in one at a time for examination by the grand jury.

(2) There is a practicing attorney among the membership of the grand jury who usually acts as the foreman. He leads off in the examination of the witnesses, exercises some control to minimize the use of evidence which would be inadmissible at the trial itself . . . and seeks to protect both the interests of the person charged and the State.

(3) A person who is charged by the State with having committed a crime punishable by death or life imprisonment and whose case is being presented to a grand jury is permitted at his own election to be present in the grand jury room while the witnesses are being interrogated. He himself may question any or all of the witnesses, though the grand jurors may not question or examine him. He may not call or present witnesses to appear before the grand jury.[11]

The quoted practices are ancient and deeply rooted in Connecticut, but they have not been emulated. Most people trained in the common law would tend to question the tendency toward "trying" accusations twice. On the other hand, there is considerable sentiment favoring at least the idea of giving the grand jury a notion of the potential defendant's story; and there is pressure for some modification in this direction of federal grand jury practice.

A sketch of grand jury activity would not be complete without some reference to their reports, often erroneously called "presentments." (A presentment is an accusation drawn by a grand jury on its own.) Reports are usually denunciations of people or organizations, frequently government officials or agencies, in situations where the grand jury finds things badly out of joint but concludes that an indictment is not permitted or justified. Until very recently, federal grand juries were not

thought to be empowered to issue such documents, but
a few judges have now ruled that in certain circumstances they are permissible. In the most famous of
these, Judge John J. Sirica upheld the power of the Watergate grand jury to issue a report regarding the conduct of then President Nixon, as well as a recommendation that it be forwarded to the House Judiciary
Committee for use in the impeachment inquiry. In addition, the Organized Crime Control Act of 1970 provides
that special organized-crime grand juries have the power
to publish reports at the completion of their terms on
certain kinds of noncriminal misconduct by appointed
public officials or employees.

On the state level, the practice is extremely varied.
Many states prohibit grand jury reports, and those that
permit them commonly circumscribe the grand jury's
power. Grand juries are generally prohibited from com-
menting on purely private activity, and reports criticizing
publicly elected officials tend to be allowed only where
statutory authority exists. Finally, as a rule, grand jury
reports may be disclosed only with court approval.

3

Selection
and Prejudice

Because the decision to prosecute is a grave one, must we not be certain that those who make it are specially qualified by intelligence, education, and overall experience? If we specify those qualifications, are we not likely to find them causes or pretexts for racial, class, sex, and other forms of prejudice? If grand juries are discriminatorily selected—all white or male or rich or respectable—will they not indict discriminatorily? But if grand juries are in the end merely rubber stamps for the prosecutor, do such questions really matter to anyone?

To answer the last question first, our law books offer proof of a steady concern with the selection and makeup of both trial and grand juries. The issues have not always been neatly logical, but the moral stakes have been high and the cases have been bitterly fought. The latest Supreme Court decision on jury composition, prohibiting Louisiana's practice of excusing women from jury duty unless they file a written request to serve, is dated January 21, 1975,[12] and it surely does not mark the end.*

From the earliest days to very recently, in keeping with a frank and fairly open tendency toward elitism, grand jurors were selected by means guaranteed to produce partiality. The poor, the racially disfavored, the young, women, and others thought inferior were at best minimally represented. The rationale relating to women, who were ineligible as jurors in England and most of this country until the twentieth century, was explained by Blackstone in proper Latin under the doctrine of *propter defectum sexus,* "because of a defect of sex." Grounds of discrimination against other groups were not explicit, in Latin or otherwise, but were no less prevalent.

Prior to the enactment of the Federal Jury Selection and Service Act of 1968, most juries were formed by the so-called key-man system: the clerk of the court or jury commissioner in a district or state would contact men of presumedly extensive community connections and request that they recommend prospective grand jurors. These jury suggestors were usually such knowledgeable and established local people as county clerks, postmasters, and school superintendents.

Although the key-man system was never declared unconstitutional, as possibly it should have been, its results were repeatedly struck down as unacceptably discriminatory. For the hand-picked grand jurors almost always came from the settled, relatively affluent, "respectable" segments of the community. Grand juries in New York City, for instance, contained in far more than representative proportions people from the middle and upper ranks of Con Ed, the telephone company, banks, brokerage houses, insurance companies, and similar establish-

---

*For a still more recent decision on discrimination in grand jury selection, see footnote on page 37.

ments. Most notably, case after case revealed racial exclusions—especially of blacks from Southern grand juries.

As a *declared* rule of law, the prohibition against racial discrimination in jury selection was made clear relatively soon after the Civil War. In 1875, Congress enacted a civil-rights law which provided that no citizen should be disqualified from jury service because of race, color, or previous condition of servitude. The Supreme Court established before 1880 that the "equal protection of the laws" guaranteed by the Fourteenth Amendment forbade systematic exclusion of blacks from jury service.

But it was not until the late '30's and the '40's that the promises of federal law and the Constitution began to be kept. In those years the High Court demonstrated its willingness to go behind state statutes guaranteeing fair jury selection and to scrutinize what was really happening. In 1939, for example, it said it was not enough for the laws of Louisiana to proclaim that in selecting grand and petit juries "there shall be no distinction made on account of race, color or previous condition [of servitude]. . . ." Where a defendant showed that *in fact* the procedures accomplished a substantially total exclusion of blacks from Louisiana grand juries, even though his *trial* jury was fairly selected, his murder conviction was reversed.[13]

A decision against Texas a year later stressed the Supreme Court's explicit resolve to deal with the realities. The Texas system of selection, through white jury commissioners, produced grand juries almost 100 percent white in Harris County, which was 20 percent black. The commissioners solemnly swore they practiced no racial discrimination. Of course, they acknowledged, they were inclined to select grand jurors from people they knew personally, and they knew hardly any non-whites. Sweeping these protestations aside, and reversing a black man's rape conviction, Mr. Justice Hugo L. Black wrote for a unanimous Court:

> What the Fourteenth Amendment prohibits is racial discrimination in the selection of grand juries. Where jury commissioners limit those from whom grand juries are selected to their own personal acquaintance, discrimination can arise from commissioners who know no Negroes as well as from commissioners who know but eliminate them. If there has been discrimination, whether accomplished ingeniously or ingenuously, the conviction cannot stand.[14]

It is a digression—but only a small and perhaps a bearable one—to note how much enmity Mr. Justice Black was to bear from fellow Alabamians for opinions like that. In his book, *My Father: A Remembrance,* Hugo Black, Jr., recounts how the whole family suffered from these recriminations. Originally, his father's nomination was opposed by the liberal community because, like many Alabama politicians of his day, he had been a member of the Ku Klux Klan. After the wheel had made its circle and the name Black had become hated in the Alabama establishment, Black's son recalls introducing him from time to time with these words: "Ladies and gentlemen, I give you Justice Black. When he first went on the U.S. Supreme Court they talked about him as a man who went around in a white robe scaring black people. Now they talk about him as a man who goes about in a black robe scaring white people."

The bitterness aroused by decisions that undid convictions for serious, often capital, crimes because back at the grand jury selection stage there had been racial discrimination was not confined to Alabama. State authorities, with some doctrinal merit, protested that an indictment is, after all, only an accusation. If the subsequent trial is fair, and a fairly selected trial jury is convinced of guilt beyond a reasonable doubt, how is justice served by allowing the grand jury's composition to upset the conviction?

The Court's answer, as articulated in a number of cases, was substantially unanimous. It was the defendant's right, the opinions said, not to have people of his race systematically excluded from either the body that accused him or the one that convicted him. The assumptions, by no means clearly expressed, seemed to include a recognition that a member of an oppressed race faced a greater chance than others of being indicted by a group composed exclusively of his oppressors.

In addition, the Court reasoned that discriminatory exclusion had a pervasive and devastating effect on the class of citizens barred from jury service, for it denied them a basic right of equal participation in the administration of justice. Branding an entire group of Americans unfit for jury service was also seen as conveying an inescapable quality of bias, regardless of whether there was any, and therefore as undermining the integrity of the legal system itself.

Of late, it has come to be held that even defendants not in the excluded group may invoke discriminatory selection to nullify convictions. In the 1975 case mentioned earlier, it was a male defendant who succeeded in having his conviction reversed by the Supreme Court because Louisiana excused women from jury service unless they asked for it in writing. Similarly, white defendants have been held entitled to complain—have been given "standing"—against systematic exclusion of blacks from serving on grand and trial juries.*

---

*As we correct the proofs of this book, the Supreme Court has just struck down a conviction in Hidalgo County, Texas, for underrepresentation of Mexican-Americans on the grand jury that indicted the Mexican-American defendant. The Court (*Castaneda v. Partida*, No. 75-1552, March 23, 1977)

It is difficult to detect in most cases the kind of prejudice courts care about where a white male defendant is indicted or convicted by a group of white males. Overall, the Court has reasoned that it is impossible to confine so narrowly the deleterious effects that flow from discriminatory grand jury selection. Reversing the conviction of a white male in a case where blacks had been excluded from both the grand jury and the trial jury, Mr. Justice Thurgood Marshall wrote for a Court plurality:

> If it were possible to say with confidence that the risk of bias resulting from the arbitrary action involved here is confined to cases involving Negro defendants, then perhaps the right to challenge the tribunal on that ground·could be similarly confined. The case of the white defendant might then be thought to present a species of harmless error.
>
> But the exclusion from jury service of a substantial and identifiable class of citizens has a potential impact that is too subtle and too pervasive to admit of confinement to particular issues or particular cases. First, if we assume that the exclusion of Negroes affects the fairness of the jury only with respect to issues presenting a clear opportunity for the operation of race prejudice, that assumption does not provide a workable guide for decision in particular cases. For the opportunity to appeal to race prejudice is latent in a vast range of issues, cutting across the entire fabric of our society.
>
> Moreover, we are unwilling to make the assumption that the exclusion of Negroes has relevance only for issues involving race. When any large and identifiable segment of the community is excluded from jury service, the effect is to

---

rejected the State's contention that the claim of unconstitutional discrimination was rebutted because the "governing majority" in the county was Mexican-American, deeming it "unwise to presume as a matter of law that human beings of one definable group will not discriminate against other members of their group."

remove from the jury room qualities of human nature and varieties of human experience, the range of which is unknown and perhaps unknowable. It is not necessary to assume that the excluded group will consistently vote as a class in order to conclude, as we do, that its exclusion deprives the jury of a perspective on human events that may have unsuspected importance in any case that may be presented.[15]

Chief Justice Warren E. Burger, together with Justices Harry A. Blackmun and William H. Rehnquist, dissented on the ground, among others, that the white defendant had shown "no credible claim of personal prejudice" to him from the racially discriminatory jury selection. The Chief Justice further complained that another plurality opinion, by Mr. Justice Byron R. White, seemed to be based on a theory that served to supply a kind of "prophylaxis against discriminatory action in all cases, regardless of any harm that might befall the accused." In the last analysis, this may well be a powerful justification for the decision the Chief Justice protested. While not necessarily satisfying either politically or intellectually, it is not uncommon for United States courts to employ a prophylactic device to achieve indirectly important ends that cannot be attained directly.

Among the most familiar (and still hotly debated) examples is the rule that evidence taken in an unconstitutional search may not be received in the trial of the person whose rights were violated. In the search case, the evidence itself (the gun, the bloody shirt, whatever) is supposedly relevant and real, properly useful toward a just conviction. Yet, the exclusionary rule seeks to deter lawless searches, not for the benefit of this or that guilty party, but to help protect the rest of us against such intrusions. By analogy, therefore, the right of minorities to serve on (or be dealt with by) juries fairly selected is thought to be more effectively enforced when any affected person, even if not himself a target of the discrimination, may raise the question and make violations of the right costly for those in positions of authority.

An almost unanimous Court used the word "prophylactic" in a different sense when it reversed the Louisiana man's conviction by an all-male jury. The opinion, written by Mr. Justice White, stressed the importance of seeking a true cross section to the degree possible, casting a cloud over devices obstructing this effort. It said:

> We accept the fair-cross-section requirement as fundamental to the jury trial guaranteed by the Sixth Amendment and are convinced that the requirement has solid foundation. The purpose of a jury is to guard against the exercise of arbitrary power—to make available the commonsense judgment of the community as a hedge against the overzealous or mistaken prosecutor and in preference to the professional or perhaps overconditioned or biased response of a judge. . . . This prophylactic vehicle is not provided if the jury pool is made up of only special segments of the populace or if large, distinctive groups are excluded from the pool. Community participation in the administration of the criminal law, moreover, is not only consistent with our democratic heritage but is also critical to public confidence in the fairness of the criminal justice system. Restricting jury service to only special groups or excluding identifiable segments playing major roles in the community cannot be squared with the constitutional concept of jury trial.[16]

Only Mr. Justice Rehnquist dissented. Unfazed by the concept of prophylaxis, he wrote:

> [The majority] concludes that the jury is not effective, as a prophylaxis against arbitrary prosecutorial and judicial

power, if the "jury pool is made up of only special segments of the populace or if large, distinctive groups are excluded from the pool. . . ." It fails, however, to provide any satisfactory explanation of the mechanism by which the Louisiana system undermines the prophylactic role of the jury, either in general or in this case. The best it can do is to posit "a flavor, a distinct quality," which allegedly is lost if either sex is excluded. . . . However, this "flavor" is not of such importance that the Constitution is offended if any given petit jury is not so enriched. . . . This smacks more of mysticism than of law. The Court does not even purport to practice its mysticism in a consistent fashion—presumably doctors, lawyers, and other groups, whose frequent exemption from jury service is endorsed by the majority, also offer qualities as distinct and important as those at issue here.[17]

To be sure, the right to serve as a juror is honored and enforced when someone is willing to take the trouble and expense to pursue it. Members of excluded groups, particularly blacks, have sued successfully to remove barriers to jury and grand jury service.[18] But this public-spirited approach is less common, for obvious reasons, than the challenge from someone prosecuted or convicted by jurors who were selected in a discriminatory fashion.

While it is unlikely that problems of discriminatory selection are all solved, the express commands of the law on the subject now seem clear and broadly undisputed. Where the federal courts are concerned, the Jury Selection and Service Act of 1968 proclaims "the policy of the United States that all litigants in Federal courts entitled to trial by jury shall have the right to grand and petit juries selected at random from a fair cross section of the community in the district or division wherein the court convenes." The Act goes on to provide: "No citizen shall be excluded from service as a grand or petit juror . . . on account of race, color, religion, sex, national origin or economic status."

To implement these salutary purposes, voter registration lists are the basic source from which jurors are drawn by chance. Being a federal statute, this law does not of its own force apply to state juries. Nonetheless, it closely approximates the rights to fair and random selection substantially enforced against the states by the Supreme Court in construing the requirement of equal protection under the Fourteenth Amendment.

None of this, it should be said, suggests that anyone has a right to a grand jury or petit jury comprising specific proportions of races, sexes, or whatever. It may happen that a particular jury selected on any day in New York City will be all white, all black, all female, or all something else. This situation will certainly bear scrutiny when it appears, but the body will be lawful if in fact it has been selected by methods that do not serve generally, and were not employed, to effect forbidden discriminations.

To this extent at least, as the law stands today, nobody is literally entitled to a jury or grand jury of his "peers," whatever that may mean. Assuming his peers have not been intentionally excluded, their absence does not invalidate the group chosen to serve.

4

Impaneling
and Indicting

Before taking up the controversies surrounding the grand jury, we think it would be useful to picture it in operation. The secrecy requirements preclude any description of "actual" proceedings, but we can work through all the steps. Since we are most intimately acquainted with the United States District Court for the Southern District of New York—the federal trial court at Foley Square that has jurisdiction over federal offenses in Manhattan, the Bronx, and several other New York counties ranging upstate toward Albany—this will be our model.

Three kinds of grand juries sit in the Southern District of New York. The first is the regular grand jury, chosen monthly, that passes on a great quantity and variety of criminal matters. Technically, it has a legal life of eighteen months; in practice, it sits for only four continuous weeks, subject to recall to complete an investigation. The second is the so-called additional grand jury that deals with lengthy and complex investigations. It serves for as long as eighteen months, but meets only one or two mornings a week. The third is the special grand jury created by the Organized Crime Control Act of 1970, which may sit for as long as thirty-six months.

Despite these differences, the selection process for all three types varies very little. And their members are drawn from the same pool of citizens gathered to supply trial juries.

Usually on the first Tuesday morning of each month in the U.S. Courthouse at Foley Square, after everyone summoned for jury service has convened in a large assembly room seating about 180 people, the jury clerk calls approximately 100 people from the room as prospective grand jurors. This group is taken to an available courtroom, where an assistant United States attorney briefly explains the nature of grand juries and the service expected from the members of the grand jury that is about to be created.

In addition, he informs the panel that a grand juror must be a United States citizen, at least eighteen years of age, and a resident of the geographical area encompassed by the Southern District of New York; he must be able to speak, read, and write English; and must have no record of felony convictions. The assistant also questions the panel to ascertain whether any members have physical infirmities, such as poor vision or hearing, that would render them unable to serve as competent finders of fact.

The next step, in the inelegant jargon of the courthouse, is the "purging" of the grand jury panel. All the names are placed in a drum, and twenty-three are pulled by the clerk for seating. Predictably, many of the people selected will have compelling reasons (business, family, health) for being excused. The Chief Judge, as part of his administrative duties, or sometimes a colleague, proceeds to purge the prospective jurors by listening individually to those who wish to be excused. As persons are excused, the names of possible replacements are taken from the drum.

Since "representativeness" is desired, purging is an early time of troubles. Active and intelligent people are liable to have jobs that don't allow comfortably for the absences required by grand jury service. There is a danger that many of those best fitted by wit and energy will be most clearly entitled to be excused. Conversely, there is a good chance that those able and willing to serve will include too large a percentage of people who are retired or otherwise without competing interests.

The balance is redressed to a degree by those whose sense of community or curiosity persuades them to adjust their busy schedules so that they can serve. Some pressure to adapt in this way may be exerted by the judge's reminders of the public need and the public interest. But the role of grand juror is not filled most effectively by a morose draftee and the earnestly unwilling are likely to be excused.

By 11 A.M. the purging is completed, leaving the group of twenty-three about to be born as a grand jury. For uninteresting reasons relating to the organization and division of the court's business, another judge will probably turn up at this point to complete the judicial midwifing, including the choosing of a foreperson and deputy foreperson.

The foreperson, or in his or her absence, the deputy, has several special tasks: to sign indictments, to swear in witnesses, to arrange absences of jury members on particular days, to give directions (most often with the prosecutor's advice) to witnesses about such matters as answering a question or returning on a given day for further testimony or producing certain records. Finally, the foreperson has a general duty to maintain order and decorum in the grand jury room.

It may be argued that the foreperson and deputy

should seem to possess a measure of administrative and leadership talent. Yet the timing and circumstances of their selection, plus the fact that they are not expected in truth to lead or command, make for a fairly perfunctory process. Not long ago, retired (white) stockbrokers and middle-management corporation types were most likely to become grand jury forepersons. Now more or less random selection is thought to be the wisest course.

At the same time, because the role of foreperson or deputy is not much sought after, many judges (including the present co-author) have found it agreeable and fair to invite volunteers. It does not happen that twenty-three hands are raised. Usually, at the first call nobody responds. Following an awkward minute or two, hands go up and the selection is made. Whether those chosen are wholly satisfactory is impossible to say. In any event, the people who step forward tend to be comfortably various with respect to race, sex, occupation, income, and related indices of special concern.

Other judges select the first two grand jurors they see for the organizational roles. Some ask whether any on the panel have had prior jury service. Still others make their selection after consultation with the assistant United States attorney. None employ standardized personnel selection techniques.

With the leadership settled, we are ready for the traditional oaths, administered by the clerk of the court. The foreperson and deputy are sworn first:

> You, as foreman [forelady] and deputy foreman [forelady] of this grand inquest, for the body of the Southern District of New York, do solemnly swear that you shall diligently inquire and true presentment make of all such matters and things as shall be given to you in charge. All of

which you shall keep secret. You shall present no one from envy, hatred or malice Neither shall you leave anyone un-presented for fear, favor or affection, gain, reward or hope thereof, but you shall present all things truly, as they come to your knowledge, according to the best of your under-standing. So help you God.

Then the other grand jurors take their oath:

You and each of you do solemnly swear that the same oath which your foreman has taken on his part, you and each of you shall well and truly observe and keep on your part. So help you God.

This done, the judge "charges" the newly impaneled grand jury. The charge, as we have mentioned, has been at various times and places a call for particular action, a stump speech for special causes of the law and against special kinds of wrongdoing, and a species of inspira-tional oratory. This last form of charge has largely disap-peared; it is certainly not the pattern in the Manhattan federal court. Here, although details and style naturally depend upon each judge, the charge is an outline of the history and functions, an introduction to the duties, and a reminder of the responsibilities of the grand jury. One can expect, too, some particular admonition about se-crecy and its importance both to protect the innocent and to help in apprehending the guilty.

Having declaimed at the grand jury, the judge departs, leaving the group in the custody of a United States mar-shal, who escorts them to one of the grand jury rooms. After distributing a handbook describing the history and duties of the grand jury (often repetitious of the judge's charge), the marshal turns the grand jurors over to the assistant United States attorney who will conduct the investigation. The panel will now take its place among as many as twenty-five grand juries functioning simultaneously in the Southern District of New York (only about seven or eight of which actively hear evidence at any given moment).

It is probably about noon on our Tuesday morning. A secretary is selected whose duties are taking attendance as well as recording the name of each witness, the matters heard by the jury, and every indictment duly voted. The assistant United States attorney explains that the quorum requirement is sixteen, that the number necessary to vote an indictment is twelve, and that the only people allowed in the grand jury room besides the jurors themselves are the prosecutor, the witnesses, and the stenographer (in New York the full proceedings are transcribed). The jurors are also told they have the right to ask questions, but that these questions should be presented to the prosecutor, who will do the asking on their behalf.

In the Southern District of New York, although regrettably not in every district, the assistant United States attorney informs the jurors of two other things: first, that if a witness exercises the Fifth Amendment privilege to refuse to answer questions because of possible self-incrimination, no inference of guilt should be drawn; second, that if the grand jury is presented with hearsay testimony, it has a right to insist the prosecution produce the witnesses having firsthand knowledge. The instructions conclude with details about the grand jury's schedule.

Upon reporting to begin hearing evidence, the grand jury is told what kind of case it will be taking up and what witnesses will testify. Laws that are presumably applicable to the facts are read and explained. This presentation, akin to an opening statement by a trial lawyer, is not transcribed.

The first witness is then called, and after the foreperson swears him in, the assistant United States attorney conducts the interrogation. When that is completed, the witness is temporarily excused and the prosecutor asks the grand jurors if they have any questions. Should he feel that a question is either improper or irrelevant, he will try to persuade the juror who proposed it to desist. Not surprisingly, the juror almost invariably complies. The witness is recalled and the agreed-upon questions suggested by the grand jury are put to him by the prosecutor.

It is not simply for reasons of efficiency that the prosecutor does the questioning rather than the jurors. His training serves to prevent the introduction of prejudicial matter that might taint the grand jury proceedings, or at least inject notes of unfairness. Not everywhere, however, are the jurors' proposed questions screened by the prosecutor. In much of New York State grand jurors are permitted to question the witnesses directly without first consulting the prosecutor. There is some feeling that this freedom gives the grand jury a sense of independence and contributes to its effectiveness as a check upon the prosecution. One state judge, early in 1976, quashed a grand jury's report because the prosecutor had refused to let the panel question witnesses directly.[19] The extent to which direct questioning actually promotes a grand jury's independence and initiative—or generates prejudice or disorder—is a subject we have not ourselves investigated or seen studied. It may well be that rigid rules, one way or the other, are unnecessary. If, as a result of possible reforms we consider later, grand jurors are made genuinely aware of their full province and powers, their acceptance of the prosecutor's guidance in putting questions may serve to maintain good order while avoiding undue constraints on their inquiries.

In any event, when the witness finishes his testimony, he is excused by the foreperson. Should there be a need for him to testify in the future, the foreperson directs him to reappear for interrogation on a specified date generally set by the prosecutor. The ordinary federal criminal case often does not involve more than a single grand jury session. Once the testimony has been heard, the prosecutor draws up a formal indictment and presents it to the grand jury for consideration. In a sort of mini-summation that is not made a part of the record, he explains why the evidence constitutes a violation of law. On occasion this is an emotional exhortation to the grand jurors to indict.

The prosecutor then departs and the grand jury deliberates in private. Unlike a trial jury, a grand jury usually reaches its decision in a few minutes and generally goes along with the prosecutor's recommendation. The foreperson signs the indictment plus another document called a "true bill," recording the number of jurors who voted to indict. At this point the entire grand jury, in the company of the prosecutor, proceeds to a designated courtroom to file the indictment by handing it up to a judge. The cumbersome business of having the grand jury file the indictment en masse is a holdover from common-law doctrine that made it a prerequisite for validity. More recent learning holds that failure to follow this ceremony will not nullify the indictment, but here, as elsewhere, rigid adherence to precedent is thought to be the better part of legal wisdom.

After checking to see that the papers are in proper form, the judge accepts the indictment, which becomes a matter of public record, and the true bill, which does not. A criminal prosecution has been initiated.

We have described broadly the normal workings of a grand jury. Prosecutors present evidence; grand juries vote; indictments are filed. The process continues for the life of the panel. As we noted earlier, few grand juries function for their full statutory terms. How long they do sit, like so many other decisions involving the institution, is exclusively determined by the prosecutor. In the case of additional and special grand juries impaneled to conduct specified investigations, such as the Watergate grand jury, their actual service ends when their investigations are concluded. A regular grand jury's work normally concludes after a month of daily sessions, when it is replaced by a newly selected regular grand jury.

5

Problems
and Prescriptions

Nobody is perfectly pleased with the grand jury. The displeasure varies with the interests and outlook of the critic—from prosecutors impatient with inefficiency and unnecessary expense to critics of the left, old and new, who see the grand jury as a weapon for prosecutorial oppression. We turn now to the major criticisms of the institution, and to some of the solutions that have been offered for answering them.

OPPRESSING CITIZENS

Notwithstanding its enshrinement in the Fifth Amendment, the grand jury for most of us is not an inviting place to sojourn. Meeting in secret, confronting the solitary witness en masse, enveloped in an aura of mystery and threat, it is bound to frighten all but the hardiest summoned to its room. Being called by a grand jury, before anything else has happened, is unnerving.

Transcending this threshold discomfort, the grand

jury, with its broad powers to investigate, may become in the wrong hands an instrument of oppression. It may seek to pry into beliefs and associations of dissident and unpopular groups where the legitimacy of its questions is unclear but the risks of resistance considerable. Since under the existing law the inquest need not define its purposes for the witness, limits on the subjects of inquiry are difficult to determine. The witness has no lawyer with him. Privileges, the right not to answer, and other legal rights known to sophisticated witnesses are not necessarily known to everyone.

The opportunity to bully, to harass, to intimidate is surely present in the grand jury room, and it has surely been exploited on too many occasions. Judge Learned Hand, never soft in matters of law enforcement, wrote eloquently of this when he dissented from a decision affirming the perjury conviction of William Remington, a government official, in a case that seems to have taken place both a long and a short generation ago.

Judge Hand refused to assent because the trial in which the perjury occurred resulted from an indictment he found to have been tainted by the intolerable behavior of a grand jury foreman and prosecutor. Remington's browbeaten ex-wife, held for long hours despite her pleas for a respite, had been sternly and falsely assured that no marital privilege entitled her to withhold secrets Remington had told her during their marriage. (As Hand observed and all lawyers would agree, she was clearly privileged *not* to tell and a court would never have allowed the testimony to be used against her ex-husband.) It was in this setting that the great judge was moved to comment:

> . . . Save for torture, it would be hard to find a more effective tool of tyranny than the power of unlimited and

unchecked ex parte examination . . . [T]he Supreme Court
has shown itself extremely sensitive to the opportunities for
oppression that such examination offers; and the present
time is hardly a propitious season to abate that vigilance.[20]

A similar warning was sounded by Mr. Justice Black
twenty or so years ago:

> Secret inquisitions are dangerous things justly feared by
> free men everywhere. They are the breeding place for arbi-
> trary misuse of official power. They are often the beginning
> of tyranny as well as indispensable instruments for its sur-
> vival. Modern as well as ancient history bears witness that
> both innocent and guilty have been seized by officers of the
> state and whisked away for secret interrogation or worse
> until the groundwork has been securely laid for their inevi-
> table conviction. While the labels applied to this practice
> have frequently changed, the central idea . . . remains un-
> changing—extraction of "statements" by one means or an-
> other from an individual by officers of the state while he is
> held incommunicado.[21]

Beyond the awesome weapon of secret interrogation,
the ability to summon people on short notice to far
places is open to abuse. Prosecutors have on occasion
employed "forthwith" subpoenas requiring the immediate appearance of the witness before a grand jury. Federal subpoena power extends throughout the nation,
and witnesses have been brought abruptly across the
country to strange surroundings when this has not been
unquestionably justified. There have been claims that
the fright and personal dislocations caused by these ex-
ertions of the subpoena power have been employed as
weapons against the unpopular. It is not necessary here
to recount the claims. Suffice to say that too many of
them have bases in fact.

Among the interests grand juries have threatened or

invaded are rights to free speech, free press, and free association, all protected by the First Amendment. Radical and nonconformist groups have depended throughout our history on the right to band together to speak and to use the printed word for dissemination of their ideas, often anonymously when disclosure of their identity could in itself chill or stifle their expressions. As the Supreme Court has said: "Anonymous pamphlets, leaflets, brochures and even books have played an important role in the progress of mankind."[22]

In a slightly earlier opinion, Mr. Justice John Marshall Harlan wrote for the Court: "It is hardly a novel perception that compelled disclosure of affiliation with groups engaged in advocacy may constitute [an] . . . effective . . . restraint on freedom of association. . . . This Court has recognized the vital relationship between freedom to associate and privacy in one's associations."[23]

The overwhelming majority of state and federal prosecutors appear to be responsible public officials obeying and enforcing the law. But in recent years some have undertaken to use or abuse the grand jury's powers to search out group relationships, originators, and participants in unorthodox political movements when legitimate law-enforcement purposes have not warranted the intrusions.

The activities of the Internal Security Division of the Department of Justice during the Nixon Administration were particularly troublesome in this respect. Often quoted by people concerned with grand jury abuses are these questions, propounded to a witness by a lawyer from the Internal Security Division before a grand jury in Tucson, Arizona, in 1970:

> Tell the grand jury, please, where you were employed during the year 1970, by whom you were employed during the year 1970, how long you have been so employed and

what the amount of remuneration for your employment has been during the year 1970.

Tell the grand jury every place you went after you returned to your apartment from Cuba, every city you visited, with whom and by what means of transportation you traveled and who you visited at all of the places you went during the times of your travels after you left your apartment in Ann Arbor, Michigan, in May of 1970.

I want you to describe for the grand jury every occasion during the year 1970 when you have been in contact with, attended meetings which were conducted by, or attended by, or been any place when any individual spoke whom you knew to be associated with or affiliated with Students for a Democratic Society, the Weathermen, the Communist party, or any other organization advocating revolutionary overthrow of the United States, describing for the grand jury when these incidents occurred, where they occurred, who was present and what was said by all persons there and what you did at the time that you were in these meetings, groups, associations or conversations.

Use of the grand jury for political purposes has evoked critical responses from the courts. In an opinion drawing some lines to protect free speech and association, a distinguished federal appellate judge, Shirley M. Hufstedler, recalled that the grand jury was provided for in the Bill of Rights because the Founders wrote with fresh memories of repressive prosecutions launched by Executive officials. Judge Hufstedler went on to say:

> Today, courts across this country are faced with an increasing flow of cases arising out of grand jury proceedings concerned with the possible punishment of political dissidents. It would be a cruel twist of history to allow the institution of the grand jury that was designed at least partially to protect political dissent to become an instrument of political suppression.[24]

Another appellate court, in a case charging members of the Vietnam Veterans Against the War with conspiring to disrupt the 1972 Republican national convention, had harsh words for the government's attempts to harass political nonconformists. In an opinion holding that it was improper for the government to name people as unindicted co-conspirators and thereby stigmatize them as criminals without providing them a forum to rebut the charges, Judge John C. Godbold, speaking for the Fifth Circuit Court of Appeals, said:

> There is at least a strong suspicion that the stigmatization of appellants was part of an overall governmental tactic directed against disfavored persons and groups. Visiting opprobrium on persons by officially charging them with crimes while denying them a forum to vindicate their names, undertaken as extra-judicial punishment or to chill their expressions and associations, is not a governmental interest that we can accept or consider. It would circumvent the adversary process which is at the heart of our criminal justice system and of the relation between the government and citizen under our constitutional system. It would be intolerable to our society.[25]

That robust language reflects awareness, along with disapproval, of the recurrent use of the grand jury merely to place selected people and groups under the investigative microscope, rather than for the neutral and impersonal business of searching after the people likely to have committed known or suspected crimes. Where the focus of prosecutive scrutiny is supposedly an organized crime figure, few have been heard to complain. In other circumstances, the procedure has been less free from criticism. When Robert F. Kennedy was Attorney General, there was spirited debate over the Justice Department's investigation and prosecution of Teamster

President James Hoffa. Detractors of Kennedy argued
that the case smacked of personal vendetta and abuse of
power. Defenders countered that Hoffa was simply the
subject of vigorous but fair prosecutive methods. Although the *bona fides* of the Hoffa prosecutions may never
be resolved to the satisfaction of all observers, the practice of directing grand jury inquiries at individuals instead of at crimes is fraught with potential for abuse of
the prosecutor's huge powers. It is certainly not unknown in human experience for a prosecutor to secure
the indictment of a particular individual because of political, racial, or personal considerations. The danger was
perceived by Attorney General (later Supreme Court
Justice) Robert Jackson in an April 1940 address to the
Second Annual Conference of United States Attorneys
(federal prosecutors):

> [The danger is that the prosecutor] will pick people he
> thinks he should get rather than pick cases that need to be
> prosecuted. With the law books filled with a great assort-
> ment of crimes, a prosecutor stands a fair chance of pinning
> at least a technical violation of some act on the part of
> almost anyone. In such a case it is not a question of discover-
> ing the commission of a crime and then looking for the man
> who has committed it, it is a question of picking the man and
> then searching the law books or putting the investigators to
> work, to pin some offense on him. . . . It is here that law
> enforcement becomes personal, and the real crime becomes
> that of being unpopular with the predominant or governing
> group, being attached to the wrong political views, or being
> personally obnoxious to or in the way of the prosecutor
> himself.[26]

The prospect of having the grand jury used as a "personal" weapon is an appalling one. There may be no
absolute safeguards against this, just as there are no

absolute protections against other perversions of the powers of government. A minimum step that might be helpful would be increasing the responsibility of judges to oversee the work of grand juries. Since the grand jury is theoretically an adjunct of the court, the courts have some power to prevent a panel's abuse or disregard of basic rights. But there is a growing consensus that additional protections are needed: rules limiting grand jury powers, codifying rights of witnesses, and adding express requirements of accountability.

THE COUNSEL CONTROVERSY

Despite its venerability, the grand jury is in many respects a mysterious institution. Except for a relative handful of specialists in criminal procedures, lawyers tend to know little of its workings. Laymen, excluding the few whose careers have made them knowledgeable, are still more ignorant and entitled to sense uncertain dangers in the grand jury room. For many called as witnesses are potential defendants and the risk of later perjury prosecutions is real. Moreover, the question of when answers are compulsory or when some valid right of silence may be claimed is often perplexing even for people learned in the law. The secret inquiry, where no impartial official presides, is obviously a situation in which the average citizen would wish to have a lawyer at hand. Yet the availability of such comfort and assistance is chancy and variable at best.

The federal courts and most states, as we noted earlier, bar counsel for the witness from the grand jury room. A national consensus does exist that a person summoned before the grand jury may have a lawyer available somewhere nearby. But like a surprising portion of grand jury lore, this is not a clearly permanent certainty. The grand jury witness is by hypothesis different from—or not yet—a defendant. He is not literally covered, therefore, by the Sixth Amendment guarantee that "the accused" in any criminal prosecution (state or federal, as the Supreme Court has held) "shall enjoy the right . . . to have the Assistance of Counsel for his defense."

This might have seemed a limited point before May 19, 1976—at least not vital for people who can afford lawyers. On that day, however, Chief Justice Burger wrote an opinion, joined by three other Justices, announcing the Court's judgment that a grand jury witness targeted as a possible defendant could later be prosecuted for perjury in his testimony without first having been told of his imperiled status, of his right to be silent, of his right to counsel, or of additional cautions known as the *Miranda* warnings.* In the course of the opinion, the Chief Justice seemed to go out of his way to observe: "No criminal proceedings had been instituted against respondent, hence the Sixth Amendment right to counsel had not come into play."[27]

Read literally, with full force and in isolation, that sentence could mean the states, Congress, or even the federal courts may bar grand jury witnesses from having any kind of assistance by counsel. Fortunately, that is not the way to read a sentence from an opinion. Elsewhere, the same opinion takes more or less for granted that a person testifying before the grand jury may have a lawyer along, if only in an anteroom, for advice. And Justice William Brennan, joined by Justice Marshall, strongly

---

*The name comes of course from the decision in *Miranda v. Arizona*, 384 U.S. 436 (1966), holding that unless the warnings are given to someone in custody as an accused, statements made by such a person under interrogation may not later be used as evidence against him.

and explicitly rejected the observation about the right to counsel. The Court's remaining members, for one reason or another, found it inappropriate to express any view on the issue.

The privilege of retaining a lawyer for a grand jury appearance, therefore, seems fairly secure. What does not currently exist is the right of someone who cannot afford to pay a fee to the benefit of assigned counsel. This, as Justices Brennan and Marshall earnestly stressed, is a notably parlous and debatable circumstance for the witness who is a prospective defendant when called to testify before the grand jury. (How "prospective" is itself a nice question; it is hardly unknown for a prosecutor in a dubious use of the grand jury to summon a person already slated for indictment in the hope of having the appearance shore up the case.)

True, the Sixth Amendment only assures an "accused" the right to counsel. But there remain the broader guarantees of the Fifth and Fourteenth Amendments, which promise, skipping a detail or two, that no person shall "be deprived of life, liberty, or property, without due process of law," or be denied "the equal protection of the laws." These provisions have been construed in recent years to mean that the right to a lawyer, an appeal, and other protections in the processes of justice may not be left to depend upon the state of the individual's bankroll. It would be a reasonable extension to hold the principle broad enough to assure an attorney's guidance for a grand jury appearance; though this is not the law at present, we would think it a civilized improvement.

Whatever happens at the federal level, the fifty states are by no means required to limit their citizens' rights to those commanded by the U.S. Supreme Court. They are free—and should act more often as if they knew it—to be more generous and libertarian than the highest court compels them to be. That is indeed part of what they could learn from Justice Louis A. Brandeis, who urged the states to function as "laboratories" for experimentation in the advancement of human welfare. In short, nothing stops a state from proceeding on its own, from its conception of the good, to supply counsel for grand jury witnesses who cannot afford to hire lawyers.

At the minimum, we think the long-time practice of the United States attorney's office in the Southern District of New York should be adopted nationally. For some years now, prosecutors in that office have regularly warned witnesses if they are "targets"—cautioning them that statements they give may be used against them, advising them of their privilege against self-incrimination, and noting their right to have counsel present in the anteroom. This, as the Supreme Court has lately affirmed, is not compulsory. It is merely decent. The voluntary course followed in New York's Southern District reminds us of what too many officials tend to forget: that the *power* to be repressive is not an inexorable mandate. Some of the highest acts of government, after all, have been uncompelled decisions to care, to be generous, and to seek justice.

Prosecutors cling jealously to the usual (albeit not universal) rule that an attorney may be available to a witness in an adjoining room, but not alongside a client in the grand jury room itself. Though the situation affords the prosecutor evident benefits of ease and freedom, its awkwardness actually produces, to begin with, annoyance and discomfort for all involved. Without a lawyer at his side, when the witness feels a particular question poses problems he must interrupt the proceedings and leave the room to consult with his counsel as to whether he must answer, how he may answer, whether to plead a privilege, etc. The very cautious witness, or one who knows he is endangered, might sensibly choose not to answer anything without consultation and proceed to write down each question as it is asked, then trot outside to discuss it with counsel. That has happened many times and could become increasingly common as people grow more wary of grand juries.

Careful lawyers have also evolved variations on the potentially exasperating shuttle after every question. One technique is to equip the witness with an alarm watch set to ring every ten minutes or so and instruct him to ask to be excused when the alarm goes off. Arriving in the anteroom, the witness dictates a summary, preferably from notes, of what has been happening in the grand jury room. The conference makes it possible for counsel to formulate objections to pending questions, to protest ambiguities in questions already covered, and to suggest clarifications or corrections in testimony already given. The alarm watch technique is not exclusive, of course; the witness may still come out at any point, with or without a ring, should uncertainties arise.

Considered with the high quota of tedium and wasted time, keeping a witness's lawyer next door is a dubious arrangement. But it is particularly questionable when one considers the attendant risks for the lay witness. Though briefed in advance, he is presumably less competent to appraise the legalities than his lawyer on the scene would be. He may be careless and do himself injury that the lawyer would have prevented. For instance, he could unwittingly delay invoking his privilege or forget to invoke it altogether, thus prejudicing his position before he is aware of the significance of his testimony.

No matter how sophisticated, the witness is at a disadvantage in the grand jury room. The prosecutor is free to examine him in any manner he chooses. The thrust of the questioning may be designed more to secure a perjury indictment than information useful to the inquiry. No judge or magistrate is there to rule on the propriety of the prosecutor's approach. If counsel were present, he would be able to advise the witness to give more detailed responses or explanations, lessening the possibility of inadvertent perjury, and he would be in a position to advise the witness when a claim of privilege is appropriate.

The mere fact that a lawyer is present may deter prosecutorial excesses that occur from time to time. In a recent case in New York State, a witness who was not represented by counsel was being vigorously interrogated by the prosecutor. Apparently unsatisfied with the witness's responses, the prosecutor accused him of "giving me baloney," of "taking me around in circles," and of "sitting there like a dummy." Stung by the prosecutor's verbal abuse, the witness unsuccessfully asked the foreman and prosecutor for an opportunity to speak with a lawyer. The transcript reads as follows:

QUESTION: Tell us generally what was said?

WITNESS: Mr. Foreman, could I please have counsel? I don't know what [the prosecutor] is trying to get me to say but I would like a counsel, please.

PROSECUTOR: Mr. Foreman, as the legal advisor to the grand jury I respectfully request that you direct that he answer my question.

FOREMAN: Would you please answer the question. . . .

WITNESS: Would you repeat it? (*The last question was read by the reporter.*)

ANSWER: I can't remember exactly what was said. . . .

QUESTION: What did you say to them?

ANSWER: I just told you what I said to them.

QUESTION: Let's go over it.

WITNESS: Mr. Foreman, please, I feel that he's badgering me too much. I would like advice of counsel, please, I'm begging you.

PROSECUTOR: I would respectfully request this witness be directed to answer the question.

FOREMAN: Please answer the question.

WITNESS: Mr. Foreman, can't I have advice of counsel? Can't I ask for an adjournment until I get an attorney here, I am not an attorney.

PROSECUTOR: Mr. Foreman, as the legal advisor to this grand jury I suggest to you that my question and my request that the witness answer the question is proper and that his request should not be granted and if I'm in error in my request to this grand jury, this witness has a remedy. As your legal advisor, I respectfully request that he be directed to answer the question.

WITNESS: Please, can't I have advice of my own counsel? I respect you for your legal ability, but I would like advice of my own counsel. I think I am entitled to that.

PROSECUTOR: Respectfully request the witness be directed to answer the question.

FOREMAN: Please answer the question. . . .

QUESTION: He didn't say to you what questions did that man ask you?

WITNESS: Mr. Foreman, please, I beg of you, I mean I don't know what [the prosecutor] wants of me or is trying to get out of me. I'm telling you what I recollect to the best of my knowledge. Now, more than this I just cannot do and if [the prosecutor] wants to continue this discussion I beg of you, I would like to have advice of counsel, please.

PROSECUTOR: Mr. Foreman, I respectfully request that the witness be directed to answer the question. I suggest to this grand jury that the question is a proper one and he be directed to answer it.

WITNESS: I'm not saying . . .

PROSECUTOR: I'm talking to the foreman now. Mr. Foreman, I respectfully request the witness be directed to answer the question.

FOREMAN: I think the question should be answered.

WITNESS: Mr. Foreman, don't I have a right to legal counsel?

PROSECUTOR: Mr. Foreman, I respectfully request the witness be directed to answer the question and the question is a proper one. Mr. Foreman, I respectfully request he be directed to answer once again.

FOREMAN: Please answer the question.

Such high-handed tactics, including the "legal advice" that the witness needs no lawyer, are presumably the exception and not the rule. Nevertheless, had counsel been present it seems likely that they would not have occurred. And if they did, the attorney could have advised his client to claim a privilege or sought assistance from the court, a course probably unknown to the unsophisticated witness.

The lawyer's presence could also help to avoid confusion, ambiguities, and derailment of the investigation. Assuming the interrogator is not aiming to confuse or mislead or trap the witness, his questions may still be vague or unintelligible, leading to answers of equal quality. Counsel for the witness, though his concerns are partisan, could expedite the inquiry by raising points about the questions and offering proposals to improve them.

Defenders of the status quo, reasoning somewhat abstractly, note correctly that the grand jury's proceedings are not adversary. Less clearly correct is their consequent contention that a witness's lawyer would inject incongruous adversarial aspects, delaying and obstructing the work of investigation. Counsel for witnesses are familiar participants in congressional hearings and in investigations by other government agencies, such as the Securities and Exchange Commission. The rules governing those situations—perhaps too strictly on occasion—have been adequate to keep them from becoming unduly contentious.

It should not be impossible to enforce similar limitations as conditions for letting counsel into the grand jury room. His role could be limited to advising the witness, and he could be prohibited from objecting to questions and arguing to the grand jury. In any event, counsel for a witness, particularly a prospective defendant, would be ill-advised to engage in obstructionist tactics that might prejudice the jury against his client. And should a witness or attorney prove disruptive, the grand jury sitting in the courthouse has the means of coping near at hand.

The second reason commonly advanced by defenders of the exclusion rule is that the presence of counsel would violate the grand jury's secrecy. The flaw in this argument is plain. There is no restriction on a witness giving his lawyer a full and detailed report of his testimony and attempting to reconstruct a verbatim transcript. Since the testimony is not meant to be secret from the witness's attorney, his hearing it firsthand is evil only if we intend him to be ineffective—a position not expressly defended by anyone.

In sum, there appears to be no genuine public benefit in barring counsel from the grand jury room. At most, the exclusion of the lawyer preserves the atmosphere of

isolation and immediate friendlessness in which the witness is questioned. But that is not an objective to be
served in the public interest.

Although the general rule still prevails, there has been
noticeable sentiment for change. The prestigious American Law Institute's Model Code of Prearraignment Procedure provides for counsel in the grand jury. The Association of the Bar of the City of New York, in its report
"Strengthening the Role of the Federal Grand Jury," has
called for adoption of the practice. The American Bar
Association has voiced its support "in principle." Samuel
Dash, who showed himself no enemy of effective investigation either as a Philadelphia prosecutor or as chief
counsel of the Senate Watergate Committee, has been an
articulate spokesman for the view that the witness has a
right to this protection.[28]

But the subject continues to inspire spirited debate.
When we first published these views in *The New Leader,*
commentators included our esteemed friend, former
United States Attorney for the Southern District of New
York Paul J. Curran. Opposing, among other things, the
idea of the witness's lawyer in the grand jury room, he
reviewed the arguments we have presented for the traditional position, plus some others that merit notice. He
wrote, for example, that lawyers appearing for grand
jury witnesses may represent others not yet called or
targeted, creating sticky problems of conflicts of interest.
Where a lawyer's "real" client is someone other than the
witness he is purportedly helping, Mr. Curran observed,
"the dangers to justice and even to the witness of a
lawyer's presence before the grand jury are manifest."
On a more somber note, he went on to say:

> I take no pleasure in noting that in the two and one-half
> years that I was privileged to serve as U.S. Attorney forty-
> one lawyers were convicted of federal felonies in the South-

ern District of New York and another eighteen were under indictment on Nov 1, 1975. Very few of these forty-one convicts have been disbarred. My point is that unfortunately one may not assume that the presence of a lawyer in the grand jury room necessarily means that the proceedings have been graced by an ethical and responsible member of the bar.[29]

Mr. Curran's criticisms, echoing those of many others, are not taken lightly. In the end, however, we must respectfully disagree. The evils he fears or recalls are, after all, matters of pathology. The lawyer-felon, or the secretly disloyal and conflicted adviser, can scarcely serve as the model on which to rest judgments of policy. If we followed comparable guides, we would have to reconsider allowing the defendant any legal assistance, even in the courtroom (a position not unheard of, but not espoused by either Mr. Curran or us). The disloyal or lawless lawyer is certainly not a boon to the administration of justice at trial. But we assume and strive for something better in the courtroom. We should proceed on similar assumptions, and strive for no less, in making the proceedings of our grand juries as fair and orderly as is reasonably possible.

INADEQUATE SAFEGUARDS

Among the other procedural safeguards reformers seek is one that would give a prospective defendant an unqualified right to testify before the grand jury. Opponents mount the familiar argument about adversary elements, supported as follows some fifty years ago by Judge Augustus Hand:

> It must be remembered that a proceeding before a grand jury is an inquest and not a trial. If defendants are treated

as having any right to be heard, the whole affair is likely to cease to be an ex parte proceeding resulting in a charge which can be fully met at the trial, but to become a litigation in which each side has the right to offer evidence, and an indictment can only be found if the evidence on the whole case preponderates against the defendants. Such it is believed was never the function of the Grand Inquest.[30]

That is the traditional view, but it may not be decisive against change. Granting the target of an inquiry the right to present his side of the story, subject to the prosecutor's cross-examination, hardly transforms the proceeding into a trial. The grand jury is not preordained to indict. It considers *whether or not* to indict. The prospective defendant may have information that would help in making that decision. Admittedly, his testimony may seldom be sufficiently persuasive to prevent indictment. But in some cases it may make a difference. Neither the grand jury nor the public at large has an interest in the return of indictments that prove—and might have been proved in advance—to be unwarranted.

A related issue is whether the prospective defendant should be able to compel the panel to hear others favorable to him. In a bank robbery case, say, he may have alibi witnesses who would place him away from the scene of the crime. The arguments pro and con parallel those on his right to testify, except that the concern about making the grand jury proceedings adversarial in nature has greater force here. Our view is that the prospective defendant should be entitled to suggest that other witnesses be called, and that the panel should have the discretion to determine what to do. This is the practice in New York State, and it appears to have worked satisfactorily there.

Along these same lines is the question of whether the

prosecutor should be obliged to present evidence to the grand jury that is favorable to the prospective defendant. At trial, the prosecutor must disclose such exculpatory evidence to the defense.[31] Only in a minority of the states, though, is he bound to make such disclosures to the grand jury.

The rationale for not insisting on "defense" evidence is again related to preventing adversary proceedings in the grand jury room. In addition, determining what is or is not or may be exculpatory is often difficult. Evidence that does not appear to be terribly meaningful to a prosecutor preparing to present a case to the grand jury may take on altogether different significance when viewed from the standpoint of the defense counsel at trial. It might place an unmanageable burden on the prosecutor at this stage to require him to discern and disclose possible matters of exculpation. At the same time, certain items, such as confession by another to the crime the target is being charged with, are so obviously exculpatory that they cannot escape notice.

Those who feel evidence favorable to the suspect *should* be disclosed point out that the prosecutor's job is not simply to indict and convict but to obtain a just result. They further argue that it is impossible for the grand jury to exercise its independent judgment as to whether criminal charges should be brought if it does not know all the facts. The American Bar Association, in its "Standards Relating to the Prosecution Function," therefore urges that "the prosecutor should disclose to the grand jury any evidence which he knows will tend to negate guilt." This standard, focused on what the prosecutor "knows" (and perhaps extending to what he *should* know), makes sense. It avoids an unrealistic duty to try the whole case before the grand jury, while demanding fairly that the grand jury, as well as prospective defendants, have the benefit of a decent concern for balance and accuracy.

We do not, however, favor *requiring* prosecutors to make such disclosures to the grand jury. A flat rule of that nature would presumably involve a remedy for its breach (including dismissal of the indictment), and would spawn more pretrial litigation than its supposed benefits would appear to justify. We believe, in sum, that as a matter of sound practice prosecutors should voluntarily disclose favorable evidence before the grand jury; we are not ready—not yet, at least—to suggest that a hard-and-fast rule be created mandating them to do so.

Contrasting with any asserted right of a prospective defendant to testify before the grand jury is the right, more commonly asserted, *not* to testify. The mere fact that someone has been identified as the target of an investigation does not prevent the grand jury from summoning him to appear and give testimony. Should a prospective defendant be informed of his possible peril so that he can make an informed judgment as to whether he should testify or rely instead on his Fifth Amendment right to silence? The answers to this question vary. In a recent opinion, Chief Justice Burger, writing for a plurality of the Court (Justices Powell, Rehnquist, and White), seemingly espoused the position that a target may be called without any special protection or formality. Starting from the proposition that "the public has a right to every man's evidence," the Chief Justice concluded that there is an absolute duty to give testimony unless the target on his own invokes the Fifth Amendment privilege:

> It is in keeping with the grand jury's historic function as a shield against arbitrary accusations to call before it persons suspected of criminal activity, so that the investigation

can be complete. This is true whether the grand jury embarks upon an inquiry focused upon individuals suspected of wrongdoing, or is directed at persons suspected of no misconduct but who may be able to provide links in a chain of evidence relating to criminal conduct of others, or is centered upon broader problems of concern to society. It is entirely appropriate—indeed imperative—to summon individuals who may be able to illuminate the shadowy precincts of corruption and crime. . . .

Accordingly, the witness, though possibly engaged in some criminal enterprise, can be required to answer before a grand jury, so long as there is no compulsion to answer questions that are self-incriminating; the witness can, of course, stand on the [Fifth Amendment] privilege, assured that its protection "is as broad as the mischief against which it seeks to guard." *Counselman v. Hitchcock*, 142 U.S., at 562. The witness must invoke the privilege, however, as the "Constitution does not forbid the asking of criminative questions.". . .

Absent a claim of the privilege, the duty to give testimony remains absolute.[32]

New York State takes the opposite view. Unlike the federal system and that of most other states, its laws provide that every witness (target or not) summoned before the grand jury automatically receives immunity from prosecution unless he has waived that protection before testifying.

A third approach, somewhere between the two extremes, was endorsed by Mr. Justice Brennan, with the concurrence of Mr. Justice Marshall, in the last quoted case. Justice Brennan pointed out that in the absence of waiver, a previously indicted defendant may not be called to testify before a grand jury about the facts of the crime of which he has been accused. By a parity of reasoning, Justice Brennan would hold that the target of the inquiry is a "*de facto* defendant" who should enjoy the same protections as a person already formally charged. It would follow that the potential defendant should be warned of his perilous position before he is interrogated:

> Thus, I would hold that, in the absence of an intentional and intelligent waiver by the individual of his known right to be free from compulsory self-incrimination, the Government may not call before a grand jury one whom it has probable cause—as measured by an objective standard—to suspect committed a crime, and by use of judicial compulsion compel him to testify with regard to that crime. In the absence of such a waiver, the Fifth Amendment requires that any testimony obtained in this fashion be unavailable to the Government for use at trial. Such a waiver could readily be demonstrated by proof that the individual was warned prior to questioning that he is currently subject to possible criminal prosecution for the commission of a stated crime, that he has a constitutional right to refuse to answer any and all questions that may tend to incriminate him, and by record evidence that the individual understood the nature of his situation and privilege prior to giving testimony.[33]

Making it necessary for the prosecutor to notify a prospective defendant of his status prior to interrogating him seems to us fair and reasonable, even if it is not compulsory under the Constitution. This is one of many situations where officers of government should readily choose to be fair without having to be coaxed. Advising a likely defendant of his situation imposes no serious burden on the prosecution and enables the witness to make a decision of critical importance with his eyes open. As mentioned earlier, the United States attorney's office in the Southern District of New York has followed this practice for some time and it has not adversely affected law enforcement.

Of course, the question when or whether the prosecutor "knows" someone is a target should not become a new source of tangential disputation. At the outset of a broad investigation in a complicated field (securities fraud or other kinds of possibly complex wrongdoing), prosecutors are likely to be unaware of some or all who may come to be accused. People may be called as witnesses who only later are perceived to be active participants in the alleged crimes. In general, the grand jury's own records should show when a particular witness has become a probable defendant. Once that identification is made, there is much to be said for informing the witness of his status.

Any witness, target or no, in any state or federal court, may exercise his Fifth Amendment privilege against self-incrimination before the grand jury. This raises the question of the prosecutor's responsibility when he is forewarned that a prospective defendant will rely on his constitutional privilege if called to testify.

At a minimum, there seems no good reason why a prospective defendant should be called and forced to claim the privilege before the grand jury. His responses, as a matter of strict constitutional law, have no meaning; nobody is supposed to draw an adverse inference from the claiming of the privilege. The only reason for the charade when it is known that the privilege will be asserted seems to be the planting of a negative inference in the grand jurors' minds, contrary to law.

The subject is handled well in a provision of the American Bar Association's previously mentioned "Standards Relating to the Prosecution Function": "The prosecutor should not compel the appearance of a witness whose activities are the subject of the inquiry if the witness states in advance that if called he will exercise his constitutional privilege not to testify." Interestingly, this was the policy followed by the Watergate special prosecutor's office. And we would add that the grand jury should not be told a target hasn't been called because he would exercise his Fifth Amendment privilege. This would have the same effect as his actually claiming the privilege before the panel. Only in those extremely rare instances where the grand jury specifically insists upon a target's appearance should the prosecution inform it of the reason for his non-appearance.

PRIVILEGE AND IMMUNITY

The problem of self-incrimination leads to the related, highly controversial subject of immunity. The Fifth Amendment protects the individual against being "compelled . . . to be a witness against himself." This means one may not be required to give testimony that could be self-incriminating—even "a link in a chain" of evidence that might pose a danger of criminal conviction.

For as long as this privilege has been recognized—including its English precursors antedating our Constitution—there have been occasions when government authorities have wanted the evidence badly enough to compel it by paying the witness with "immunity" from prosecution. Where this protection is of sufficient scope, the witness cannot rely upon the privilege to legitimate his refusal to testify; he must answer or he may be imprisoned, or otherwise punished, for contempt.

It has been said that the immunity is not a fitting exchange for the privilege. The right not to answer, the argument runs, is given to protect the dignity and privacy of the individual. The pain and ugliness of confessing to a crime are not erased by the assurance of non-prosecution.

Whatever its merits, and it obviously has some, the argument has not prevailed. The grant of immunity, always provided it is of requisite breadth, is enough to force testimony. As the Supreme Court recently explained: "The existence of these [immunity] statutes reflects the importance of testimony, and the fact that many offenses are of such a character that the only persons capable of giving useful testimony are those implicated in the crime."[34]

Controversy has raged, however, over the dimensions of the immunity that must be granted. The focus lately has been on the difference between "transactional" and "use" immunity. Described briefly, transactional immunity protects against prosecution for any of the transactions or occurrences that are subjects of the compelled testimony. Use immunity forbids only later use against the witness of either the evidence he has been forced to give or evidence derived from his testimony. In fuller shorthand, the latter is better denominated as "use and derivative use" immunity.

To illustrate: If a grand jury witness testifies under compulsion about a particular bank robbery, having been granted transactional immunity, he cannot later be prosecuted for that bank robbery. If he has received only use immunity, he may be prosecuted later for the bank robbery, but the immunity prevents use of his grand jury testimony or of leads that are derived from it in the prosecution.

In May 1972, upholding a statute enacted two years earlier, the Supreme Court ruled that "use and derivative use" immunity is an adequate constitutional exchange for compelled testimony because it is "coextensive with the scope of the privilege."[35] The privilege, the majority of the Court declared (Justices Douglas and Marshall dissenting, and Justices Brennan and Rehnquist not participating, producing a 5–2 vote), "has never been construed to mean that one who invokes it cannot subsequently be prosecuted."[36] In opposition to this view, it was argued that use immunity leaves the witness exposed to the danger of new evidence being found and used against him as a result of leads, new witnesses, and new information that would not have been obtainable without his compelled testimony. The Court handled this by holding that in any later case the burden would be upon the prosecution to prove the absence of such "taint" in the additional material it proposed to introduce as evidence.

Nonetheless, the debate goes on. Before the 1970 law, Congress had repeatedly provided for transactional immunity, and proposals now before the House would revive this policy.

There has also been discussion lately over whether immunity should be a two-way street, open to the defendant as well as to the prosecution. A legal scholar, Peter Westen of the University of Michigan Law School, has mounted a substantial case for the position that defendants ought to have the right to require immunization of witnesses who could help their defense but who take the Fifth Amendment. He begins with the right of a defendant under the Sixth Amendment "to have compulsory process for obtaining witnesses in his favor." In the light of that, Westen writes, there are arguments at least as powerful for immunizing defense witnesses as for giving immunity at the behest of the prosecution. After all, the immunity is not now against prosecution of the witness; it only prevents the subsequent use of the compelled testimony, or leads from it, against him. While the prosecution, if it later proceeded against the witness, would have to show it had relied on independent sources for its evidence, that is no worse than the burden shouldered by the government when the immunity is requested for its own benefit. As Westen puts it:

[T]he inconvenience is no greater than when the prosecution grants immunity to its own witnesses. If convicting the guilty justifies immunity for government witnesses, exonerating the innocent should justify immunity for defense witnesses. The public interest in each case is to determine the truth, and the standard for granting use immunity in each case should be the same, namely, whether it is "necessary to the public interest." Once the state makes immunity available to the prosecution it should not be permitted arbitrarily to withhold it from the defense.[37]

The contention has force. But for the time being immunity is an essentially exclusive prosecution weapon, and it is likely to be a good while, if ever, before the courts or the legislatures give defendants access to that weapon. Great store will probably still be placed in the proposition that immunity favors the witness who gets it; that the resulting "sacrifice" of potential prosecutorial power requires a balancing of *governmental* interests; and that private parties, unfettered by the prosecutor's overall concerns, could use the power of immunization casually and irresponsibly to shield guilty witnesses from the law.

In the present climate, developments on this issue, as on other legal matters, are likely to be modest rather than dramatic, involving small adjustments and compromises. A possible stimulant to change could be a case where prosecution use of immunity, coupled with denial of the device to the defense, touches the judicial nerve that hurts at the sight of seemingly blatant inequalities. This was suggested in a 1966 opinion of Judge Burger (some three years before he became Chief Justice of the United States), writing for the District of Columbia Circuit Court of Appeals. The defendant in a narcotics case had requested that the court direct the prosecution to grant immunity to a prospective defense witness who was a participant in the crime. Judge Burger declined the invitation, reasoning that such a procedure should be legislatively rather than judicially created:

> What Appellant asks this Court to do is command the Executive Branch of government to exercise the statutory power of the Executive to grant immunity in order to secure relevant testimony. This power is not inherent in the Executive and surely is not inherent in the judiciary. In the context of criminal justice it is one of the highest forms of discretion conferred by Congress on the Executive, i.e., a decision to give formal and binding absolution in a judicial proceeding to insure that an individual's testimony will be compelled without subjecting him to criminal prosecution for what he may say. The effect of the immunity grant avoids any incrimination. The Government does not suggest that Congress could not provide for a procedure giving a defendant a comparable right to compel testimony, but only that Congress has not done so. Whatever the merits of the arguments in favor of such a procedure, it is obvious that it would require safeguards to preclude abuses; the complexity and difficulty of evaluating the impact of that course suggest at once the inadequacy of the facilities available to the judiciary to make the assessment. We conclude that the judicial creation of a procedure comparable to that enacted by Congress for the benefit of the Government is beyond our power.[38]

Judge Burger did, however, leave open the possibility of judicial intervention in cases of obvious unfairness where the government's actions are less than even-handed.

> We might have quite different, and more difficult, problems had the Government in this case secured testimony from one eyewitness by granting him immunity while declining to seek an immunity grant for Scott to free him from

possible incrimination to testify for Earl. That situation would vividly dramatize an argument on behalf of Earl that the statute *as applied* denied him due process. Arguments could be advanced that in the particular case the Government could not use the immunity statute for its advantage unless Congress made the same mechanism available to the accused. Here we are asked in effect to rewrite a statute so as to make available to the accused a procedure which Congress granted only to the Government.[39]

While the perplexing subject of immunity is not easy to resist, its possible use for defense witnesses is something of a byway for our subject; the question, in its nature, is one that arises almost exclusively at trial, not in the grand jury. As we have noted, historical and practical reasons militate strongly against turning grand jury proceedings into adversarial contests. Yet there is, as we have also mentioned, a discernible movement among some reformers to require that prosecutors be compelled to disclose to the grand jury evidence that tends to undermine their case. And that, though it may be in the relatively distant future, could raise questions as to whether the immunization of witnesses before the grand jury should serve prospective defendants as well as the prosecution.

SECRET PROCEEDINGS

Government lawyers have fought with religious fervor to maintain the secrecy surrounding grand jury proceedings. The wall has been coming down in recent years, but very slowly. It is only lately in the federal courts that a defendant has become entitled to a copy of his own grand jury testimony. The testimony of other witnesses is generally not available to a defendant unless they are called to testify at his trial. The secrecy is probably still overdone, but there are genuine problems in trying to modify it.

When the Supreme Court in 1956 said pure hearsay or otherwise incompetent evidence—that is, evidence that would not be received over objection at a trial—would be enough to sustain an indictment, one underlying concern was avoiding the prospect of having "trials" over the "sufficiency" of the evidence before a grand jury. That basic worry remains substantial.

Yet the traditional view, restricting access by a defendant to grand jury minutes, makes our criminal justice system less progressive than most of us would like to believe. Three decades ago, Mr. Justice Jackson pointed out that at the Nuremberg war-crime trials (where he served as chief American prosecutor), the Soviet Union's legal representatives complained that the limited disclosure allowed in American practice was unfair to the accused:

> The Soviet Delegation objected to our practice on the ground that it is not fair to defendants. Under the Soviet system when an indictment is filed every document and the statement of every witness which is expected to be used against the defendant must be filed with the court and made known to the defense. It was objected that under our system the accused does not know the statements of accusing witnesses nor the documents that may be used against him, that such evidence is first made known to him at trial too late to prepare a defense, and that this tends to make the trial something of a game instead of a real inquest into guilt. It must be admitted that there is a great deal of truth in this criticism. We reached a compromise by which the Nuremberg indictment was more informative than in English or American practice but less so than in Soviet and French practice.[40]

While the Soviet (and general European) practice of opening prosecution files to the defense has not been adopted here (for reasons that reflect other differences, good and bad, between the different procedural systems), a number of our states are freer in revealing grand jury minutes than are the federal courts. In some states a defendant is permitted to inspect the grand jury minutes as a means of raising the point that the evidence the grand jury heard did not warrant an indictment. For that purpose, the secrecy ends after the indictment has been voted.

On the federal level, however, the Supreme Court has found it wise to enforce secrecy as a means of blocking inquiries into the adequacy of grand jury evidence. Much can be said for this stance, whatever its flaws as a matter of strict logic. The grand jury's question is whether or not to *accuse.* It is not handled in an adversary fashion. The sufficiency of the evidence is not contested. The defendant, after indictment, gets a full opportunity to test the evidence before the trial jury. It is at the least highly doubtful that this should be preceded by a trial of the grand jury's decision to indict.

To be sure, being indicted is a grave blow in itself. The injury ought to be inflicted only after due deliberation on a record responsibly judged to be adequate. Still, the cure of testing the grand jury's evidence is likely to be worse than the disease, slowing still further, and for reasons less than compelling, a criminal process that already aggravates the community by its pattern of tortuous and leisurely complexities.

Granting all that, the insistence upon sealing grand jury minutes seems excessive, for they may serve legitimate needs of the defendant. The defendant may be thinking of calling at trial a witness who has testified before the grand jury, and he would obviously benefit from having the record in trying to make an informed judgment. The grand jury testimony, gathered through the powerful resources of the government, may contain leads to other helpful witnesses or documentary evidence. It may support defense positions in ways neither the prosecution nor the judge can know, even if they intend in good faith to deliver exculpatory materials.

Admittedly, there are difficulties. Some defendants may tamper with witnesses or with their own stories if they are given access to the full grand jury record. But this should not be a general or decisive presumption. In the handful of states where a defendant is permitted pre-trial discovery of the entire grand jury transcript— California, Iowa, Kentucky, Minnesota, and Montana— there is no evidence so far of any higher incidence of obstruction of justice or subornation of perjury than in the rest of the states. And where there is an actual risk of harm to witnesses, the court can issue a protective order limiting disclosure.

The tide flows in favor of disclosure. We may expect to see increasing movement in that direction, assuming, of course, that minutes exist to be examined. Most courts do not require stenographic recording of grand jury proceedings. The minority practice is clearly preferable; there appears to be no good reason why it should not be universally mandated.

A related problem is the witness's (as opposed to the defendant's) right to a copy of his own testimony. As we have seen, grand jury secrecy arose initially for the protection of witnesses, not for the benefit of the state. Professor John H. Wigmore, the leading expert on evidence, concluded that the right to have grand jury testimony disclosed or not belongs to the witness:

> The privilege, therefore, is not the grand juror's, for he is merely an indifferent mouthpiece of the disclosure. Nor

is it entirely the state's, for the state's interest is merely the motive for constituting the privilege. The theory of the privilege is that the witness is guaranteed against compulsory disclosure; the *privilege* must therefore be *that of the witness,* and rests upon his consent.[41]

Since the witness is probably the best judge of whether he requires the protection of grand jury secrecy, it can be persuasively argued that the choice should be his. There are situations where the witness requires the benefit of access to his prior testimony. Should he be summoned before another grand jury or regulatory body inquiring into the same matter, or be asked to testify for the defendant at trial, the witness would desire sensibly to review his prior testimony. In short, we favor changing the usual practice that denies a grand jury witness a transcript of his testimony.

LEAKING INFORMATION

Just as there is on one side a problem of too much secrecy, there is on the other a problem of too little. Grand jury "leaks" are a recurrent and steadily nagging concern. It should be clear on principle that these violations of the rules are evil.

True, there are times when the claims of principle dim in the light of immediately attractive objectives. The citizen's reaction to leaks from the Watergate grand jury, or involving Congressman Mario Biaggi or Spiro Agnew, will depend upon his view of the particular victim at the particular moment. Nonetheless, a reasonably clear principle obtains here: The casual assassination of character or impairment of status through the illicit breach of grand jury secrecy ought to be seen always as a wrong, to be prevented when possible and punished when appropriate.

Leaking of grand jury minutes, whether by prosecutors, stenographers, or jurors themselves, is punishable on the federal level as contempt of court and in New York State as a misdemeanor. Unfortunately, this power is too seldom employed. In New York State there is no record of the sanction having been applied in a case of improper disclosure of grand jury minutes. Given the ever-increasing number of prejudicial leaks emanating from grand juries throughout the land, it is clear that the sanction has been without effect.

It would perhaps be more effective if Congress enacted a specific statute making it a crime to leak grand jury materials, and allowing victims to collect money damages without proof of actual damage. Such an approach would provide the necessary warning and certainty which should characterize the criminal law. It also might be appropriate to provide that anyone convicted of this crime could be removed or suspended from public office. Bar associations can play a role in preventing leaks, too, by taking disciplinary action against offending attorneys. In any case, better sanctions are needed to restore secrecy to the grand jury.

ADVERSE PUBLICITY

We live in an age when the media have a profound impact on our perceptions of people and issues. Investigative reporters have repeatedly sensitized public opinion to the existence of abuses in the body politic and the need for reform. Although the price is sometimes high, most of us favor freedom of expression. Whether we do or not, the First Amendment has survived and, with some vicissitudes, grown over the years.

Among the costs and difficulties generated by a free

press is the recurrent problem of the publicity attending some indictments. If the defendant is famous or notorious, or the alleged criminal conduct brutal or extensive, public interest (meaning, in the first instance, media interest) is high. The indictment in such a case is likely to be the occasion for detailed press releases and the holding of press and TV conferences by the prosecutor.

Too many times the show for the media includes well-publicized arrests of the defendants where law enforcement personnel (supposedly operating under tight "security") are accompanied by a battery of newspaper and television photographers. The whole extravaganza is a threat to fair trials. The process cannot be transformed utterly while we preserve a free press, but it could be modulated and controlled far better than it is.

Judges regularly instruct trial juries that indictments have no evidentiary weight and that no inference of guilt may be drawn from them. The instruction is deeply meaningful, underlining as it does the presumption of innocence and the prosecution's burden of proof beyond a reasonable doubt. Yet, in the eyes of most newspaper readers, an indictment is a long step toward condemnation. Should the accused ultimately be acquitted, the publicity is generally a good deal less prominent and may never quite remove the stigma of the earlier treatment.

Why does the prosecutor hold a press conference at all to announce an indictment? There is, we are told, a public "right to know." But is it not—or could it not be —served by a routine filing of indictments in the courthouse press room, leaving it for the journalists to decide what is hot, cool, or tepid? One answer is that an indictment may need to be explained a little—though many of those most publicized are not complicated. Another is that the prosecutor, like other public officials, should not be inaccessible to the press—quite apart from the personal urges that have tended to make inaccessibility a small problem.

On balance, we think responses to media inquiries are certainly legitimate, but the prosecutor's press conference to announce (celebrate?) an indictment serves no valid purpose. It ought to be forbidden.

A related issue concerns media reports that someone has been subpoenaed to testify before the grand jury. The reading public, more often than not, concludes that the witness must be involved in the wrongdoing that is the subject of the grand jury's probe. Actually, of course, that is far from universally true. Many a person is summoned merely as a witness and not because there is any reason to believe he or she is guilty of any misconduct. Even where a witness is in fact the target of the inquiry, frequently no indictment is returned because the evidence is found wanting.

In those situations, it seems fair to provide some means to bring the truth to the public's attention. California has recently passed a law providing that the target of a probe ending without indictment may request the grand jury to announce "that a charge against such person was investigated and that the grand jury could not as a result of the evidence presented find an indictment." It provides as well that an individual summoned solely as a witness may request the grand jury to declare he or she "was called only as a witness to an investigation which did not involve a charge against such person."[42]

The California statute represents a commendable approach. In some instances a public announcement of vindication may serve to refresh dimmed memories or inform those previously unaware of the fact that a person was involved in a grand jury inquiry. But the choice, and the weighing of the pros and cons, is given to the individuals directly affected. Many, especially those in public life, will welcome the opportunity to quell unfounded charges and rumors. Moreover, the law may serve to deter prosecutors from leaking information that can later be shown, to their discredit, to have been erroneous.

TRIAL BY REPORT

A grand jury "report," as we explained earlier, is an account of an investigation and findings, usually accusing people of misbehavior, but not indicting anyone. Whether these reports should be permitted has been a subject of perennial debate, and knowledgeable champions are found on both sides. Those favoring reports have included Thomas E. Dewey, Richard H. Kuh, and former Chief Justice Arthur Vanderbilt of the New Jersey Supreme Court. Among those opposed are Federal District Judge Edward Weinfeld and spokesmen for the American Civil Liberties Union and the American Bar Association.

Supporters say reports perform the important task of alerting the community to neglect, inefficiency, and misconduct in government where it does not rise to the level of a crime. They consider this vital for mobilizing public opinion behind necessary reforms and holding public officials accountable. In this vein, former New York County District Attorney Kuh, author of a leading article on the issue, has argued:

> Proper use of the grand jury's inquiring and reporting functions may mark the resurgence of that body as an important factor in effective government. At the same time, such use will protect the citizenry from the tyranny of improper accusation. These have been historic grand jury

functions, somewhat neglected in the misinterpretation of that body's history and in the grand jury's preoccupation with the quasi-mechanical operations of handling routine indictments.[43]

Those who disagree respond that grand jury reports are tools for official character assassination by a body of essentially irresponsible amateurs without recourse for the victims. The critics also point out that one of the purposes of grand jury secrecy is to protect the reputation of any individual under investigation whose conduct does not justify a criminal charge. This protection, the critics argue, is undermined when reports are issued naming those against whom there was insufficient evidence to warrant indictment. The opponents' position has been stated in a frequently quoted New York case:

> A presentment is a foul blow. It wins the importance of a judicial document; yet it lacks its principal attributes—the right to answer and to appeal. It accuses, but furnishes no forum for a denial. No one knows upon what evidence the findings are based. An indictment may be challenged—even defeated. The presentment is immune. It is like the "hit and run" motorist. Before application can be made to suppress it, it is the subject of public gossip. The damage is done. The injury it may unjustly inflict may never be healed.[44]

Grand jury reports have also been attacked because the jurors lack the expertise to comment properly on the performance of government agencies and programs. As Judge Stanley H. Fuld put it:

> Grand jurors are not selected for their skill in appraising efficiency in public office or delving into matters more appropriately reserved for executive or legislative action. . . . Moreover, the secrecy which necessarily surrounds the

action of the grand jury prevents fruitful debate as to the merit of its charges, and the immunity which surrounds its members removes the normal restraint against recklessness. Under these circumstances, there is grave danger that grand jury reports may as readily be used as instruments of unfair partisan politics as of public enlightenment.[45]

It seems clear, in short, that grand jury reports pose grave dangers of largely unanswerable character assassination, amateur criticism of governmental action, and the general evils of vigilantism. Bearing the imposing seal of the grand jury, they are fierce weapons, not weakened at all by the popular misunderstanding of their possibly ignorant origins.

But the evidence of history is not all on one side. The grand jury as a roving ombudsman has a fairly long and frequently honorable record. In modern times, some reports have been instruments of healthful exposure and reform. Few, for example, have been heard to quarrel with the report of the Watergate grand jury.

Of a piece was the 1970 report of a Maryland grand jury that exposed possible corruption relating to federal construction projects and involved high public officials. In that case, the grand jury had voted to indict, but the Department of Justice refused to sign the indictment, preventing prosecution. The publication of the draft indictment as a report opened the dispute to probably desirable public scrutiny.

On the other hand, many reports have been ill-conceived, unfair, and simply destructive. In 1952, a New York grand jury investigated possible violations of the perjury and conspiracy laws by union officials who had filed affidavits with the National Labor Relations Board affirming that they were not members of the Communist Party. No indictments were returned. But the grand jury filed a report declaring that a number of union officials had in fact been Communists and had invoked the Fifth Amendment when questioned about their affidavits. The affidavits of these men were therefore worthless and a "subterfuge," the grand jury said, and recommended that the NLRB revoke the certification of the unions they represented. In addition, the foreman of the grand jury and an assistant United States attorney leaked the names of the union officials to the press. Fortunately, Judge Edward Weinfeld ordered the report expunged, a decision not less notable for the fact that one Senator Joseph McCarthy was riding high at the time.[46]

Our tentative view, though not very heroic, is that reports should be returned only where the subjects are public officials, where there are compelling reasons, and where the grand jury has reached substantially unanimous and significant conclusions. Employed sparingly, as a kind of residual power of the people, this device to bring evils to public attention may produce benefits worth the effort and some risk.

The grand jury should not compete in this work with other agencies of government unless they are quite plainly delinquent or corrupt. If the device is used too often, the forces opposing reports altogether are likely to have their way. If it is used with wisdom, the case for total proscription is not overpowering.

ACCUSATIONS WITHOUT TRIAL

Conspiracy indictments often identify some individuals as "unindicted co-conspirators." Of uncertain origin, this practice until recently has been generally accepted, but it raises some of the same problems associated with grand jury reports.

Proponents, primarily prosecutors, say the naming of unindicted co-conspirators has the salutary effect of giving the trial jury (and the public) the full picture of the alleged misconduct. They assert that there are instances where participants in a criminal scheme are not, as a practical or legal matter, open to criminal prosecution due to such factors as immunity, death, or pardon. More important, they contend that because the acts and statements of all participants in a conspiracy are admissible in evidence against the indicted defendants, the indictment must name the unindicted co-conspirators.

Opponents respond that those named as unindicted co-conspirators are subjected to an accusation of criminality without any opportunity to disprove it. As a result, reputations are damaged and employment opportunities lost. According to these critics, all too frequently people are named as unindicted co-conspirators, though the evidence is insufficient to prove their guilt, because they have refused to assist the prosecution. It is unnecessary, these critics correctly note, for an indictment to specify the unindicted co-conspirators before the prosecution may utilize evidence of their acts and declarations at trial. This information can be supplied later in a "bill of particulars," which lacks the judicial appearance of the grand jury accusation, is usually not accompanied by the public fanfare associated with an indictment, and, unlike an indictment, may be shielded by a protective order that preserves the reputation of those not indicted.

The propriety of naming unindicted co-conspirators has lately come under critical judicial scrutiny. The case of the Vietnam Veterans Against the War, cited in our earlier discussion of "Oppressing Citizens," involved seven men charged with conspiracy to disrupt the 1972 Republican national convention. Three others were

named as unindicted co-conspirators. Two of these petitioned the trial court to delete the references to them in
the indictment. After being rebuffed by the trial judge,
they brought their complaint to the Fifth Circuit Court
of Appeals. In a strongly worded opinion, the Appeals
Court granted their application. The court found no legitimate governmental interest that was furthered by
"stigmatizing private citizens as criminals" while at the
same time "denying them a forum to vindicate their
names."[47] It was unimpressed by the government's
claimed need to name unindicted co-conspirators so that
it could take advantage of their statements and acts at
trial:

> The government may introduce evidence at trial of a per-
> son's participation in a conspiracy and thereby ascribe his
> acts and statements to the co-conspirators even if that per-
> son is not named in the indictment. . . .
>
> An unindicted conspirator anonymously designated as an
> "other person" or as "John Doe" may be unmasked in a bill
> of particulars or at trial. The bill of particulars is, however,
> the statement of the prosecutor and does not carry the
> imprimatur of credibility that official grand jury action does.
> At least arguably its public impact may be tempered by
> protective orders entered by the court. When a witness tes-
> tifies at trial he does so as a private individual and makes no
> formal adjudication regarding criminality. An indictment,
> the formal act of an impartial, formally convened quasi-
> judicial body of historical status and power, carries more
> impact on the reputation of its subject than does trial testi-
> mony. In any event, it must be recognized in the process of
> balancing private injury and governmental interests that
> wholly different, and valid, governmental interests apply to
> naming the private citizen in a bill of particulars or in trial
> testimony than apply to identifying him in the indictment as
> an unindicted co-conspirator.[48]

The court's approach seems sound. It achieves a worthwhile social end at very little cost. There may still be occasions when the naming of unindicted co-conspirators serves valid purposes without the prejudicial effects of the quoted case—for example, where such individuals have already been charged with a crime arising out of the transactions encompassed by the conspiracy, or have escaped indictment by agreeing to give incriminating testimony as part of a bargain with the prosecution. Nevertheless, without some showing of special need, the prohibition against the practice is wise.

It is not possible to leave this issue without mentioning the controversy engendered in 1974 by the naming of President Nixon as an unindicted co-conspirator in the Watergate cover-up case. Because there was a substantial question as to whether an incumbent President could be prosecuted, or as a policy matter should be, the Watergate Special Prosecutor did not seek to indict President Nixon. The grand jury did, however, identify him as an unindicted co-conspirator—although this was not contained in the indictment as returned but was recorded in the grand jury minutes for later disclosure.

After President Nixon refused to comply with a subpoena for his tape recordings, the Special Prosecutor relied on the grand jury's finding to uphold the validity of the evidentiary demand. When the matter reached the Supreme Court, the President's lawyers argued that the grand jury lacked the power to name an incumbent President as an unindicted co-conspirator. They claimed that only the House of Representatives, as part of the impeachment process, could accuse the President of participation in a criminal conspiracy. Hence, they asserted, the grand jury's action was improper and could serve only to prejudice unfairly the President's rights in the pending impeachment process.

The Special Prosecutor countered that the grand jury was empowered to charge conspiracies that included co-conspirators who were not legally indictable. In such circumstances, the argument went, the grand jury was not precluded from alleging, and the prosecution not precluded from proving, the participation in the criminal scheme of persons who, for legal, constitutional, or practical reasons, were immune from prosecution, including the President of the United States:

> In short, the jurisdiction of the grand jury to name unindicted co-conspirators is a necessary part of the power to charge defendants in a conspiracy case and is not restricted by any immunity a co-conspirator may enjoy not to be brought personally before the bar of justice to answer for the offense.
>
> There is, we submit, no reason to make an exception for an incumbent President. We realize that the President is entrusted with awesome powers and responsibilities requiring his full attention. While indictment would require the President to spend time preparing a defense and, thus, would interfere to some extent with his attention to his public duties, the course the grand jury has followed here in naming the President as an unindicted co-conspirator cannot be regarded as equally burdensome. It is regrettable that the thrust of the evidence in the grand jury's view encompasses an incumbent President, but it would not be fair to our legal system or to the defendants and other unindicted co-conspirators to blunt the sweep of the evidence artificially by excluding one person, however prominent and important, while identifying all others.[49]

The Supreme Court bypassed the opportunity to answer this unique and esoteric question when it ordered Mr. Nixon to surrender the tape recordings. Despite this gap in the law, it is to be hoped that the opportunity will not arise again.

HARASSING SUSPECTS

If a defendant is found "not guilty" at trial, he may not be tried again for the same offense. The concept is enforced as part of the constitutional protection (also in the Fifth Amendment) against "double jeopardy."

Double jeopardy has no applicability, however, to the grand jury. Having failed to obtain a true bill from one grand jury, the prosecutor is usually free to re-present the case to a different panel with the hope of success (subject to local variations, as in New York, where court authorization is required for the second effort). This stirs some basic notions about fairness—and unfairness. The grand jury is scarcely independent of the prosecutor as it is. Why, then, should it be possible for a panel's infrequent dissent to be nullified by a more compliant grand jury? Doesn't that institutionalize rubber-stamping?

Not always. In some circumstances re-presentation may be reasonable. Prosecutors, like many other civil servants, are often overworked. They may not prepare for a grand jury presentation with the intensity of preparation for a trial on the merits. All the available evidence may not be produced; witnesses may not be completely debriefed as to their knowledge of the transactions under investigation; leads and clues may not be fully explored. Consequently, a case where there is probable cause may fail initially to win the grand jury's favor. And there is no compelling societal interest in freeing someone who has committed a crime simply because, to paraphrase Mr. Justice Cardozo, the prosecutor has blundered. At least, it may be argued, not when the blunder occurs before the suspect has been exposed to public accusation and trial.

The issue is interesting, albeit not one that arises too frequently. Having failed once, prosecutors do not generally try again without good reason. There does not appear to be much concrete evidence of prosecutorial abuse or harassment in the form of successive presentations to different grand juries. Our tentative view is that the case for change here remains to be made.

ALLEGED BIAS

The days of blatant discrimination in grand jury selection on grounds of race, class, or religion seem now fairly well ended. By and large—certainly in the federal courts and probably in just about all the states—the names for grand jury service are chosen in random fashion from voter registration lists.

But there remains the charge that grand juries are unfairly constituted because identifiable groups, particularly those most often affected by the criminal process, are underrepresented. Specifically, it is argued that minorities, the young, and the poor are not proportionately represented on voter registration lists and this is reflected on jury panels.

Although the assertion seems correct, it has not stimulated a mass movement for change. One reason is the difficulty of proposing a better selection method. Where people are free to register (if they are not, that is an independent basis for legal relief), it does not appear unreasonable to ask that much interest in public affairs as a condition for grand jury service. Were something other than voter registration lists to be employed, truly random selection would become complex and old practices of bias might reappear in new forms. Thus, the attack on the use of voter registration lists is weak both on its intrinsic merits and in the absence of preferable substitutes. The lame character of the position is apparent from the self-contradictions of one otherwise thoughtful writer, who says on this subject:

> . . . A broader base than voter registration lists is obviously necessary. Of course, any qualified juror, even if not registered to vote, may volunteer for jury service. Perhaps an increased awareness that government is choosing to use the courtroom as an arena of confrontation with political dissidents will give rise to a new understanding of the importance of jury service and will spur juror registration drives among the disaffected and disenfranchised, similar to the voter registration drives of the Sixties.[50]

WEAPON OF THE PROSECUTION

A small cluster of disparate critiques center on the evident fact that the grand jury is controlled by the prosecutor. To be sure, the notion of the institution as a shield for the innocent—presumably at the heart of the reasons for its inclusion in the Bill of Rights—is continually echoed in judicial opinions. Relatively recently the Supreme Court stated:

> Historically [the grand jury] has been regarded as a primary security to the innocent against hasty, malicious and oppressive persecution; it serves the invaluable function in our society of standing between the accuser and the accused . . . to determine whether a charge is founded upon reason or was dictated by an intimidating power or by malice and personal ill will.[51]

Apt as that description may have seemed for the People's Panel in the eighteenth century, it certainly is not much realized in practice in the twentieth. This has even been recognized by the Department of Justice. In a letter written in September 1974 to Chairman Peter Rodino of the House Judiciary Committee, then Assistant Attorney General W. Vincent Rakestraw observed:

> Possibly the most cherished rationale for the grand jury system is that it protects the individual against the prosecutor's "partisan passion or private enmity.". . . . Whatever may have been true many years ago when the nation was less populous, it is highly questionable today whether any such protection for the individual is realized by having grand juries. Today the Federal prosecutor relies generally upon the investigative agencies to develop cases, and he will never previously have heard of the defendants in most of the matters presented to him. Then, too, the grand jury performs a purely preliminary function; the proceedings are ex parte; only 12 members need agree that probable cause exists to indict while as many as 11 members may disagree; and the return of a no bill does not preclude further efforts by the prosecutor to establish basis for indictment. In that light it is certainly doubtful whether the grand jury system provides the individual any surer protection than that afforded him by the prosecutor's own sense of civic and professional responsibility and his certain desire to perform fairly and competently in the sight of the bench, the bar and the public.

The contemporary grand jury investigates only those whom the prosecutor asks to be investigated, and by and large indicts those whom the prosecutor wants to be indicted. As federal judge William J. Campbell points out:

> Today, the grand jury is the total captive of the prosecutor who, if he is candid, will concede that he can indict anybody, at any time, for almost anything, before any grand jury.[52]

In the same way, those the grand jury "refuses" to indict are likely to be people the prosecution does not want indicted. Many of the cases ending with a "no true bill" are actually instances where a prosecutor feels the need for such backing to support his own view that further proceedings should not be held.

There is nothing necessarily sinister in this. On the contrary, some cases in which a "crime" has literally been committed—the youthful seducer of a female legally too young to consent; the impulsive, seemingly one-time shoplifter—are for one reason or another difficult for the law-trained official to overlook. The grand jury's dispensing power, kin to the power of a trial jury to acquit the technically "guilty," supplies some needed play in the joints of a system not always supple. But saving graces of this sort do not alter the fact that the grand jury rarely stands in the path of a prosecutor determined to indict. Perhaps it is not realistic to hope for anything sharply different. Indeed, few reformers urge the serious pursuit of this theoretical function.

On the other hand, there is active dissatisfaction that the grand jury seldom does *more* than the prosecutor asks. It is possible that Watergate, at least temporarily, has added impetus to this sentiment. Rightly or wrongly, it was thought that the Washington grand jury was not being led to sweep broadly or dig deeply in the months before the first trial at which Judge Sirica presided. It appeared to at least some observers that if not for the unusual circumstance of the judge himself insisting upon more intensive inquiries, profound misdeeds might never have come to be prosecuted.

Whatever may emerge as the exact truth about the Watergate proceedings, there is considerable sentiment for stressing to grand jurors when they are impaneled that they possess powers for investigative efforts independent of the prosecution—that they may require witnesses to be called and documents to be produced, may refuse to hear witnesses introduced by the prosecution, and may ask questions as extensively as they wish. Reformist voices have also called for strengthening the grand jury's ability to initiate inquiries into criminal offenses on its own. The main concern, again seemingly reflective of Watergate, is providing it with the authority and personnel for investigating possible wrongdoing by the Executive branch. If limited to acts of government as opposed to crime generally, this proposal may merit serious consideration.

PERJURY—DETECTED OR PROMPTED

Our legal system is premised on the disclosure of the truth leading to fair and just results. A trial is often said to be a search for the truth. The extent to which we genuinely pursue that ideal is debatable, but it is a prized value. Witnesses who testify in any judicial proceeding, whether before the grand jury or at trial, "swear to tell the truth, the whole truth, and nothing but the truth." Those who violate that oath are subject to the substantial penalties attached to the crime of perjury. As Chief Justice Burger recently pointed out:

> In this constitutional process of securing a witness' testimony, perjury simply has no place whatever. Perjured testimony is an obvious and flagrant affront to the basic concepts of judicial proceedings. Effective restraints against this type of egregious offense are therefore imperative. The power of subpoena, broad as it is, and the power of contempt for refusing to answer, drastic as that is—and even the solemnity of the oath—cannot insure truthful answers. Hence, Congress has made the giving of false answers a criminal act punishable by severe penalties; in no other way can criminal conduct be flushed into the open where the law can deal with it.[53]

While few people condone lying, critics of the grand jury system (and of the prosecutors who run it) complain that the apparatus is misused to snare unwary witnesses on perjury charges. All too often, it is said, people are summoned before a panel solely to obtain a perjury indictment rather than to discover information about pre-existing criminal activity. Perjury charges should not be brought, these critics argue, if the supposedly false testimony relates to transactions that are not crimes, or if the criminal activities about which the witness is questioned occurred so long ago that prosecution for them is barred by the statute of limitations.

Although the argument has force, it has failed to gain acceptance. The grand jury need not restrict its probes to events that constitute prosecutable crimes. It can inquire into any past matters that may provide leads for the investigation of suspected criminal activity not barred by the statute of limitations. And a perjury prosecution may be based on any false testimony that has "a natural effect or tendency to influence, impede, or dissuade the Grand Jury from pursuing its investigation."[54] If a truthful answer to the grand jury's question could conceivably have furthered its investigation, a prosecution for perjury may be brought.

These principles are illustrated in a case from the strange era of Prohibition, still cited with some regularity for its legal doctrine as well as for its qualities of comic opera. In 1926, a party was held at the Earl Carroll Theatre in New York City. Earl Carroll testified before a grand jury investigating whether alcohol had been served in violation of the law and was indicted for perjury. The proof at trial established that

> . . . at the party and on this occasion, a bathtub which had been standing at the side of the stage was moved to the

center of the stage and that the [defendant] came to the
center of the stage and stood by the bathtub. A Miss Hawley
came from the wings, dressed in a chemise. The [defendant]
held a cloak in front of her while she slipped from the
chemise and got into the bathtub, whereupon the [defend-
ant] announced that "the line forms to the right; come up,
gentlemen." About 15 or 20 men lined at the side of the
bathtub, and as they passed by, took glasses and filled them
with the contents of the bathtub. Thereupon, the bathtub
with the girl still in it was pushed back on the stage. There
was testimony that the liquor which was put into the bathtub
came from a small keg and that it was a beverage. Witnesses
testified that they drank glasses of champagne taken from
the bathtub.[55]

Carroll was found guilty, but he was not convicted of
lying about whether champagne had been served. Instead, his perjury related to his denial that anyone had
bathed in the tub, an act that was not in itself a crime—
certainly not a federal crime. The Court of Appeals rejected Carroll's argument that a perjury conviction could
not be based on such false testimony:

> The questions addressed to the [defendant] were evi-
> dently inspired by a widespread publication of newspaper
> stories of the champagne bath given to a nude woman at a
> party at the Earl Carroll Theatre on the night in question.
> When summoned, the questions addressed to the [defend-
> ant] were undoubtedly conceived for the purpose of learn-
> ing who was there, so that others might be summoned as
> witnesses. The identification of the woman who stepped
> into the bathtub might also serve to produce a witness. A
> false statement as to the woman tended to mislead the
> Grand Jury, and to deprive them of knowledge as to who she
> was, so that she might not be obtained as a witness. The
> Grand Jury has it within its power of investigation to ascer-
> tain the names of all possible witnesses. . . .

Clearly, one who stepped into the bathtub, by smell, sight, or taste, could testify as to whether or not it contained champagne, thus the materiality of the testimony is made clear. . . .

The bathtub had been used as a container of beverage, but the perjury was about the girl who was in the bathtub, which was independent of the beverage contents. The spectacular immersion of Miss Hawley in the tub, standing alone, was inconsistent with the story of the [defendant] before the Grand Jury. Her stepping into the tub with 15 or 20 men passing by drinking from it to her health became a material matter in the investigation whether or not there was a violation of the Volstead law. The Grand Jury's investigation was to determine whether intoxicating liquors had been possessed or furnished at the party. [Defendant's] effort was to conceal such a violation.[56]

And so it remains to this day. A witness may be guilty of perjury for lying about a "material" fact, however innocent or noncriminal that fact may be on its own. The rule is potent, yet it makes sense if the grand jury, entitled to range broadly in its inquiries, is to have truthful responses that will assist its inquiry and not intentional falsehoods likely to derail the investigation.

Nevertheless, there are instances where the prosecutor is forewarned as to the witness's testimony and, believing it will be false in light of other evidence he has secured, summons him anyway for no other purpose than to obtain a perjury charge. This tactic raises basic questions of fairness and propriety. The witness pursued in this fashion can scarcely be said to have been called for the ostensible purpose of aiding the grand jury's investigation. The useful information is already known. If not technically "entrapment" in the strict sense of that legal term, the setting of the stage for what the prosecutor hopes will be perjury is close kin to such forbidden "creation" of crimes. Where prosecutors have engaged in such conduct, they have sometimes been held to have passed even the wide boundaries of their powers in the grand jury room.

In one instance, an employee of the Internal Revenue Service was questioned before the grand jury about his recollection of a meeting that had occurred four years earlier. Prior to testifying, he had given an affidavit to a government investigator in which his account of the meeting differed from that of the three other participants. Not unexpectedly, he testified the same way before the grand jury and was indicted for perjury. The case was extraordinary in that the defendant appeared to have been hauled to Nebraska for no other apparent purpose than to extract perjury from him. The Court's pronouncements are apposite here:

> The Court is of the opinion that the evidence in this case clearly established that Mr. Newcomb's [the prosecutor] purpose was simply to do what he did, viz., to extract from defendant his testimony about the talk in which he had taken part in St. Louis on May 3, 1950, knowing that his recollection of it differed from that of the others present, and to get him indicted for perjury. He knew how each of the parties to that talk, including the defendant, remembered it because each had made his sworn statement to investigator Strain, and three of the parties to the talk had already given their recollection of it to the grand jury before Newcomb called defendant. Extracting the testimony from defendant had no tendency to support any possible action of the grand jury within its competency. The purpose to get him indicted for perjury and nothing else is manifest beyond all reasonable doubt.[57]

That case is a rarity in our law, as probably it should be. The evil of perjury remains major. It is not widely to be "excused" because the opportunity to commit it may have been afforded by an avid prosecutor. Nor do we desire our relatively infrequent perjury trials to be burdened too regularly by trials of the prosecutor—to see whether he expected, looked for, or was otherwise not surprised by, the lies.

The best hope in this quarter, if by no means a thorough safeguard, is that we have prosecutors busy enough with important matters, and decent enough, to refrain from summoning people to testify for the sole purpose of securing a perjury charge. There is enough criminal activity already existing to keep even the most industrious and able public prosecutor fully occupied. That important work should be vigorously pursued. Prosecutors overreach and oppress when they employ the grand jury process itself as a creator of crimes.

"RUNAWAY" GRAND JURIES

In the federal courts (and in the many states with similar laws, constitutional or statutory), there can be no prosecution for a felony except under a grand jury's indictment. That much is clear and simple enough.* Consider, though, the situation where a grand jury wants to pursue alleged wrongdoers and the prosecutor does not share the desire. Can the grand jury indict on its own? Can the prosecutor drop a case the grand jury has seen fit to initiate? How do such conflicts arise? Who resolves them?

---

*Of course, nothing in the law (or, for that matter, in life) is utterly clear and simple. A qualification here, though not momentous, is that a federal defendant (as again in many states) may "waive" indictment—i.e., agree that a felony prosecution may go forward against him merely on a written accusation by the United States attorney. This is a relatively rare procedure, reflecting the common privilege to forgo a constitutional right. But, except for such a voluntary relinquishment, presumably for some good reason, the right stands.

Questions like these generate some fascinating and still remarkably unsettled problems of law and government. They arise infrequently, which accounts in part for the continued absence of definite answers. Usually, the familiar fact of the prosecutor's control covers the subject. It is the rare grand jury that thinks itself of indicting, or is led by someone other than the prosecutor to indict. If there has been an indictment and the prosecutor decides to drop it, the grand jury has no effective voice in the matter. Unless a judge interferes, the prosecutor's decision to dismiss or file a *nolle prosequi* will end the case.*

Yet there are still the occasional cases that test our principles. Before recalling a couple, we should note a few of the principles that do not solve, but help to formulate, the hard questions. First, it is pertinent to have in mind that the prosecution of crimes is normally deemed an *Executive* function, specifically the prosecutor's, and in the federal sphere this normally means the United States attorneys, subject to the overall supervision of the Attorney General. Second, as a corollary, we start with the generally enforced premise in our law that there is a very broad range of prosecutorial *discretion*—of final authority in the prosecuting establishment to decide, without interference or supervision by any other organ of government, whether to prosecute or not.

Such principles have their roots in the Constitution. Article II proclaims and assigns the Executive power. The Chief Executive is to see that the laws are "faithfully executed." And as the Supreme Court has said: "The Attorney General . . . is the hand of the President in

---

*Another qualification: a defendant may object, and may succeed in his objections. Where an indictment is to be dismissed only with a view to bringing another one at some other time or place, the result may involve harassment. If a judge is persuaded of this, the dismissal will be denied.

taking care that the laws of the United States in protection of the interests of the United States in legal proceedings and in the prosecution of offenses, be faithfully executed."[58]

Another corollary follows quickly: To find something in Article II (the Executive power) and not in Article I (Legislative) or III (Judiciary) is a matter of prima facie significance under our constitutional scheme, specifically in terms of the sometimes nebulous doctrine of the separation of powers. Neatly put again in the prepotent words of the Supreme Court (from a day when our certainties, as voiced by Mr. Justice George Sutherland, were perhaps more certain than they have become), the "general rule" is tidy and uncomplicated:

> It may be stated then, as a general rule inherent in the American constitutional system, that, unless otherwise expressly provided or incidental to the powers conferred, the legislature cannot exercise either executive or judicial power; the executive cannot exercise either legislative or judicial power; the judiciary cannot exercise either executive or legislative power. The existence in the various constitutions of occasional provisions expressly giving to one of the departments powers which by their nature otherwise would fall within the general scope of the authority of another department emphasizes, rather than casts doubt upon, the generally inviolate character of this basic rule.[59]

All that could mean—and has sometimes been said to mean—that the Attorney General, or, usually, the United States attorneys, have unreviewable, final, and exclusive power to decide who will and who will not be prosecuted. But, like all broad sweeps in the law, this one is too broad. At the outset, remember, the prosecutor cannot prosecute without the grand jury. Immediately, the neatly compartmented, "separated" powers are blurred by the Constitution itself; for the grand jury is thought to be an organ of the *court* (Article III), not the Executive.

And that is only a beginning of the possible complexities. For, though they seldom occur, perplexing and dramatic cases sometimes arise when the several main participants—prosecutor, grand jury, and judge—disagree about whether a prosecution should properly be instituted or dropped. Take, first, the matter of beginning a case. As we now know, the grand jury has an absolute veto over whether to indict. Does the same apply to the prosecutor? So-called runaway grand juries in state courts have succeeded from time to time in bringing prosecutions without the aid, or even over the opposition, of the regularly designated prosecutor.

So, too, special prosecutors have been appointed where the regularly elected or appointed officials have failed to act. As noted earlier, the corrupt political machine of Boss Tweed in New York City was successfully pursued by a grand jury that acted independently of, and in spite of, the district attorney. Some fifty years later, Thomas E. Dewey was appointed special prosecutor in New York City because of the seeming nonfeasance of the regularly elected district attorney.

Such unusual cases characteristically involve matters of bitter conflict in the community. Like most "hard" or "great" cases, they tend to make somewhat special, unique, or possibly "bad" law.* In any event, state courts remain unclear, and perhaps are shifting even now, on whether judges have the power to appoint special

---

*Holmes, all lawyers recall, said "great cases like hard cases make bad law" —*Northern Securities Co. v. United States*, 193 U.S. 197, 400 (1904) (dissenting) —meaning somewhat peculiar law, tortured to achieve an immediate objective, not safe or sound or good for application in the general run of "normal" cases.

prosecutors to pursue cases the grand jury, but not the regular prosecutor, deems appropriate.

In the federal picture, the court-appointed special prosecutor has been substantially unknown. In recent times, a federal rule of criminal procedure—not constitutional law, of course, but still binding generally until it is changed—has required that an indictment be "signed by the attorney for the government." (Another rule requires the signature of the grand jury foreman as well.) This sounds like an inescapable and unambiguous barrier to the grand jury's proceeding without that attorney. But people learned in the law have seen means of escaping and possibly overriding barriers that appear insurmountable at first. While the barriers here still stand, the debate may not be over.

Way back in 1964, when the civil-rights movement was rumbling through the South and all of the nation, a federal grand jury sitting in Mississippi thought it should indict for perjury two black witnesses for the government in a voting-rights case against a Mississippi registrar. The United States attorney, under instructions from then Acting Attorney General Nicholas DeB. Katzenbach, respectfully said otherwise, and refused either to prepare or to sign any such indictment.

District Judge Harold Cox sided with the grand jury. (He had in a sense initiated the prosecution when, during the voting-rights trial, he stated that "these Negroes" should be "bound over to await the action of the grand jury for perjury.") After giving the United States attorney an hour to relent, Judge Cox held him in contempt and ordered him into custody. He directed further that the Acting Attorney General should hie himself to Mississippi and show why he too shouldn't be bound over.

The government appealed Judge Cox's order to the Fifth Circuit Court of Appeals. That court reversed the

ruling, but it was a close and not quite resounding reversal. A majority of four of the seven judges went narrowly
on the ground that the prosecutor's decision not to sign
an indictment cannot be countermanded by a district
judge—more precisely, that the judge lacks power to
order the United States attorney to sign. A different majority also agreed that Judge Cox had rightly ordered the
United States attorney to help the grand jury *draft* the
indictment, despite his being free not to sign it.

Three dissenters thought this erroneously overlooked
the historic range of the grand jury's powers, and that
the prosecutor's signature, a mere "authentication," is
(1) not vital and (2) compellable anyhow by the judge
because it is a "ministerial" (not discretionary) act. But
even these three took the position that the United States
attorney, having signed, could refuse to go forward in
the prosecution of the indictment, and that the court
would lack the power to alter that stance or impose punishment for it. Judge John Minor Wisdom, voting against
Judge Cox across the board, said:

> Against the backdrop of Mississippi versus the Nation in
> the field of civil rights, we have a heated but bona fide
> difference of opinion between Judge Cox and the Attorney
> General as to whether two Negroes, Goff and Kendrick,
> should be prosecuted for perjury. . . .
> This Court, along with everyone else, knows that Goff and
> Kendrick, if prosecuted, run the risk of being tried in a
> climate of community hostility. They run the risk of a pun-
> ishment that may not fit the crime. The Registrar, who pro-
> voked the original litigation, runs no risk, notwithstanding
> the fact that the district court, in effect, found that [the
> Registrar] did not tell the truth on the witness stand. In
> these circumstances, the very least demands of justice re-
> quire that the discretion to prosecute be lodged with a per-
> son or agency insulated from local prejudices and parochial

pressures. This is not the hard case that makes bad law. This is the type of case that comes up, in one way or another, whenever the customs, beliefs, or interests of a region collide with national policy as fixed by the Constitution or by Congress.[60]

Those expressions suggest why four opinions in that troubled situation may not represent the last words on grand jury versus prosecution powers.

A second case of interest that found its way to the Fifth Circuit came in the legal torrent after Watergate. On February 6, 1974, Jake Jacobsen, onetime friend of Nixon Administration Treasury Secretary John B. Connally, was indicted by a federal grand jury in Texas on seven counts of fraudulent dealings with a savings-and-loan association. In May of the same year, Jacobsen told Watergate prosecutors in Washington he had made bribe payments to Connally, agreed to plead guilty to a bribery charge, and agreed to give testimony for the prosecution. In return, the prosecutors agreed to "dispose of" the Texas action. (Jacobsen later did testify against Connally, who was acquitted.)

To carry out the deal, government attorneys sought to dismiss the Texas indictment. The *state* attorney general objected, declaring he had delivered evidence to the federal people with the understanding that his "relinquishment of such investigatory data would not have taken place had the State of Texas not believed that the ends of justice would be fully pursued" in the federal prosecution.

Moved by this, among other things, District Judge Robert M. Hill denied the government's application for dismissal. The government responded by filing a "Notice of Intention Not to Prosecute." Judge Hill fired back with an order appointing two special prosecutors to go ahead with the case. The government appealed, taking as its legal handle the appointment of the special prosecutors, which was said to exceed the powers of the district judge.

The appeal, as the opinion was to reflect, loosed Olympian issues of constitutional law. The Attorney General chose as his first line an argument that always sounds like a thunderbolt; he asserted the "absolute power" of the prosecutor (the Executive branch) to dismiss an indictment, denying any judicial power whatever to question or hinder. But claims of absolute power are discordant in the judicial ear; perhaps predictably, the argument was not accepted in anything like its full dimension. Instead, the issue was found to center upon a federal Rule of Criminal Procedure that says: "The Attorney General or the United States attorney may by leave of court file a dismissal of indictment . . . and the prosecution shall thereupon terminate."

The question in one sense was whether the words "by leave of court" in that rule signified that the prosecutor had to persuade the court before a dismissal could be allowed. On the higher level to which the appeal rose, the question was whether that rule could *constitutionally* limit the Attorney General's claim of absolute power. "The question," the court observed with some solemnity, "is squarely presented here for the first time as a controversy between the Executive and Judicial Branches of government involving opposing asserted powers under the Rule." It followed, said the court, that the Judiciary must decide, scarcely pausing over the now familiar, but still possibly bemusing, proposition that judges sit on their own cases, as it were, when the problem concerns their powers versus those of another branch. In accustomed style, the opinion paid its respects to what some (or indeed almost everybody in most other countries) might find anomalous. It said: "Surely, we should approach our task with the humility which characterizes the proper exercise of all power."

Humbly, then, the court rejected the Attorney General's sweeping position, but on grounds that declared him victorious in the case, so that the declaration of judicial authority was scarcely a blow or a crisis. The court does indeed have some say, it was held, as to whether the prosecutor may dismiss the indictment. For one thing, the court must protect defendants against possible harassment and oppression by successive filings of indictments and dismissals—a problem hardly presented in the case under consideration. More broadly, however, the court affirmed the existence of an "essential judicial function of protecting the public interest in the evenhanded administration of criminal justice without encroaching on the primary duty of the Executive to take care that the laws are faithfully executed." Limiting that generality a little, the court reaffirmed that the prosecutor's discretion to proceed or dismiss should normally be decisive: "The exercise of its [the Executive's] discretion with respect to the termination of pending prosecutions should not be judicially disturbed unless clearly contrary to manifest public interest." Viewed in this light, District Judge Hill's refusal to let the prosecution end was held to be unjustified, and his decision was reversed.[61]

The practical upshot seems to be that prosecutors can end prosecutions substantially without judicial interference unless some plain impropriety or dereliction is discovered. The reserved judicial power stands as a cautionary sign, a warning that there may always be a demand for an explanation and an exposure of the prosecutorial decision to public view. If not momentous, the limitation seems a healthy one. It may be added that the precise scope of the limitation is not marked in concrete; new cases and new problems may yet lead to new dimensions. On the other hand, cases like Jacobsen's are rare in the extreme; the usual response of a judge to a prosecutor's decision to withdraw an indictment is likely to be relatively unquestioning acquiescence.

In a word, we may expect in the foreseeable future that there will be few runaway grand juries and few instances of interference by judges with the prosecutor's plenary control over decisions to begin or withdraw criminal cases. The exceptions will probably arise in situations of uncommonly deep and bitter conflict—where alignments are not predictable and it is not possible to know in advance whose will be the voices of the good or bad guys.

For that among a host of reasons, the precise lines of grand jury and prosecutor authority may never be drawn with finality. The uncertainty has to date been reasonably tolerable. It may even be healthful for the pertinent law to stay a little loose and incomplete, rather than try to freeze an unknown future too hard too far in advance.

6

Abolition
or Reform

At the time of our writing—in fact, as a primary reason for our writing—there is a substantial amount of public concern about the roles and uses of the grand jury. There are widespread charges, and not a little proof, of abuses. The grand jury has served too often, as we have noted in earlier pages, to harass the unorthodox and the unpopular. Its large and secret powers have proved too frequently to be terrifying weapons in the hands of righteous or cynical prosecutors. There have been too many cases in which witnesses have been badgered, trapped, subjected to harsh, sudden, and wearing appearances in distant places, defamed by leaks not necessarily accidental, or otherwise scarred by gratuitously high-handed or perverse employment of the grand jury's great authority.

The rise of vocal and informed dissatisfaction is, of course, a wholesome phenomenon in a democracy. There is, as we write, an array of thoughtful bills in the Congress, and comparable measures in some of the states, designed to cure the perceived disorders. The proposals reflect, and have in turn generated, careful

study of the issues and the choices. The main justification for books like this one is the attempt to supplement
the resources for knowledgeable action by the people
through their representatives. To serve that purpose, it
seems useful to identify the main lines of proposed
change in the law, to note key value choices that appear
to be in the offing, and to state some of our own prefer-
ences among the available options. This last is less important, we think, than our effort to state what the options are and what they mean.

The most sweeping design for change remains, of
course, the still powerful body of opinion that favors
abolition of the grand jury. The effort proceeds not only
in the states but also in the Congress, where abolition
would require amending the Fifth Amendment, a revision which, it should be noted, would be the first change
ever made in any part of the Bill of Rights. However
heady, the attempt is being made. From time to time
proposals have been advanced, in one form or another,
for altering the Fifth Amendment so as to eliminate the
grand jury entirely or leave it available only as an op-
tional arm for the Congress, or perhaps the Executive,
to enlist in times of perceived need as an added
prosecutorial resource.

The effort to alter the Fifth Amendment encounters a
deep-seated conviction among many constitutional lawyers and scholars that it is dangerous to tamper with any
part of the Bill of Rights, which has remained exactly as
it was adopted nearly two hundred years ago. Any
change, it is often suggested, may be the start of fatal
breaches. The entire panoply of cherished protections—
of speech, religion, privacy, due process, and the rest—
is thought to be jeopardized once the process of revision
is started and is seen to be acceptable. The idea is
weighty. There is surely a heavy presumption against

revising a set of guarantees to the individual that has become so deeply rooted and vital a part of our national heritage. At the same time, one may question the proposition that every clause in the Bill of Rights must be held changeless for all time. The Republic would stand if, for example, the uncertain "right of the people to keep and bear Arms" (Second Amendment) or the assured right of jury trial in every common-law case "where the value in controversy shall exceed twenty dollars" (Seventh Amendment) were to be altered, or even abolished. Apart from such relatively minor items, the whole Bill of Rights, like other human inventions, must remain open for critical appraisal from time to time, even granting that an enormous task of persuasion is assumed by proponents of change.

We conclude, after our own reflections, that the heavy burden of justifying an amendment to eliminate the grand jury has not been sustained. If the grand jury disappears, the "indicting" function, or its analogue, will exist elsewhere. So, too, will the investigative function, including the power to compel testimony and the production of evidence. The case is yet to be made that alternative devices are sure to be better in vital respects.

In that regard, it should be re-emphasized that among the most important sources of present unhappiness with the grand jury is the problem of abusive, intimidating treatment of witnesses. If, as we assume, some investigative agency or person (a magistrate, a "one-man grand jury") would be needed and empowered to interrogate people, there is the prospect of questioning, very possibly under oath, in some office or chamber or hearing room, with or without counsel.

The danger of browbeating could well be greater in such circumstances than it is before the grand jury. A group of twenty-three citizens, not professionally wedded to the law enforcement machinery, may still serve as a moderating influence on impatient or intemperate officials. The salutary presence of concerned laymen remains a source of potential benefit in the grand jury as well as in the petit jury.

We should not reject lightly the role the grand jury plays in providing a vehicle for citizen participation in government. The grand jury and trial jury are the only institutions in our judicial system in which nonprofessionals are involved in the decision-making process. In a time of growing skepticism among our citizens that government is responsive to their needs, the grand jury provides a mechanism for ordinary people to play a role. The process is sometimes cumbersome. Professionals are more "efficient." But the values of such amateur struggles are familiar and substantial.

The role of the amateurs is, or can be, much more than strictly cosmetic. Any experienced prosecutor will attest to the reliance he places on grand jurors' reactions to the credibility of a witness, and to the persuasiveness of a novel or complex prosecutive approach in making a judgment about whether a case should be pursued.

For all the disappointments, then, and all the resulting skepticism, we wind up believing that the ancient institution is worth preserving, largely in the interest of values that have been its professed, if frequently unrealized, justifications. The tribunal can still serve, as it was meant to, as a protection for the individual against official zeal and callousness. It remains potentially valuable for keeping the people and their law somewhat in touch with each other. And it may function yet as a source of the flexibility and the humanity that professional law enforcers tend sometimes to overlook.

If it is to remain vital and worthy, however, the grand jury needs improvement—in some respects perhaps a return to the older, better ways. And this is where the main energies of law reformers, at least on the federal scene, have been bent in recent years. To a large extent, pending proposals deal with problems that have been canvassed in earlier pages of this book. It seems useful, nevertheless, even at the cost of some repetition, to draw things together in this final chapter by reviewing the major provisions currently being considered and bringing into focus our views on these and some proposals of our own.

Instructions by judges. In the olden days, the impaneling of a grand jury was often an occasion for high, and highly political, oratory by the judges. The process has tended to become dry and routine in current practice. The judge's "charge" to the grand jury is likely to be brief (no vice in itself), formal, and uninstructive. Some judges omit it altogether. Bills pending in Congress would require a partial return to the older style, and this seems desirable.

There is no reformist pressure favoring a revival of judicial involvement in partisan combat. The objective is to advise the new grand jurors more effectively of their broad authority, and of the duties to their fellow citizens for which the authority is conferred. The judge would be required to inform the grand jurors in some detail about their powers over witnesses, documents, and other evidence, as well as about the subjects to be investigated, the nature of immunity, and other powers to be administered by the panel. The main objective would be to give the citizens being impaneled some sense of their independence under law—not to incite unguided adventurism, but to underscore the necessity for positive judgment rather than supine obedience to the prosecution.

At least one pending bill would enforce by robust

sanctions the judge's duty to give adequate instructions. It would permit a witness not to testify before a grand jury that had not been properly instructed. Still more severely, the bill says a defendant would "be entitled to a dismissal of any indictment by such grand jury and of any indictment issued by any other grand jury, if such other indictment is based on the same transaction, set of transactions, event, or events."[62] This last proposal strikes us as overkill. It is not good to lose sight of the underlying interest in seeing that the criminal law is enforced, which includes bringing to trial people against whom there is probable cause. That interest is undervalued by providing that an accused may avoid prosecution altogether, after a prosecutor and a grand jury have found there is enough evidence to submit to a trial jury, solely because a judge at a prior stage has failed to inform the grand jury sufficiently of its duties and powers.

This is not to depreciate the desirability of adequate instructions. Indeed, the opportunity to improve in this respect ought to be seized by judges now, without awaiting or needing legislative commands. It should certainly be supposed that the improvement will be attempted without further prompting by judges who help to write books about grand juries.

Prosecutorial accounting. Another proposal would require the Attorney General to report annually to Congress and the Administrative Office of the United States Courts on the work of federal grand juries. The statements would contain statistical information on investigations, requests for immunity, contempt citations, arrests, indictments, no-true bills, etc. Presumably these data would be available for future grand jury reform.

The reporting idea should be adopted and arguably extended. The grand jury is officially an arm of the court, but judicial supervision has been minimal. United States attorneys and district attorneys should be required to inform the court regularly about the grand jury's work. The practice might produce effective guidance and supervision, and might allow judges to make the grand jury a more meaningful agency of the court concerned with interests beyond prosecution. It would make for better understanding by the judges of current complaints and dissatisfactions, whether to attempt remedies or, in proper cases, to sustain the prosecutor against his critics. Possibly of greater importance, it might give pause to the occasional prosecutor tempted to act in ways that would not sound attractive in his required report.

Keeping records. Closely related to the reporting requirement is a suggested rule that would demand a transcript of all that goes on in the grand jury room except the grand jurors' private deliberations. This would include not only the testimony of witnesses but instructions and directions by the prosecutor before and after the taking of testimony. The knowledge that a record is being kept is a sobering prophylactic against casual, slipshod, or malevolent behavior. There is no inconsistency with the interest in secrecy. The transcript would remain sealed, as it commonly is in current practice, until a legitimate need arose to consult its contents.

A bill of rights for witnesses. Probably the main impetus for reform has been a widening belief that grand juries are frequently used in oppressive and punitive ways against persons called as witnesses. Several suggestions, most of which seem sound to us, take aim at these abuses.

RIGHT TO COUNSEL. For reasons cited earlier, we share the mounting sentiment that a witness should be permitted to have a lawyer with him in the grand jury room to advise him there and then of his rights and liabilities. Granting that the Constitution has not been interpreted to require it, we would favor a law providing a lawyer at public cost to any grand jury witness who claims he cannot afford to retain one. We have considered the argument that a lawyer for the witness would delay and obstruct the grand jury's work. The argument is not weightless. The writers have experience, from self-appraisal as well as from observation, that exemplifies the capacities of lawyers to delay and obstruct in the perceived interests of their clients. The remedy, however, in the grand jury as elsewhere, is not to deny altogether the assistance of counsel, which is often the result of barring the lawyer for the witness from the grand jury room. The remedy is to regulate the counsel's role—a kind of control familiar and effective in the courtroom, legislative hearings, and administrative proceedings. It would require a combination of remarkably ineffectual prosecutors and judges to defeat the efficacy of such supervision.

DECENT NOTICE. Except in rare conditions of emergency, a witness should have some minimal notice—a week or ten days—before a compelled appearance to testify. Knowledgeable witnesses, especially business people involved in investigations of economic crime, routinely have adjournments arranged beyond the customarily brief time between the service of a subpoena and the date on which it commands their appearance. The ignorant and the disadvantaged lack this modest luxury. There is usually no good reason for the abrupt summons.

DISTANCE. A potential for terror, or added terror, is the grand jury subpoena requiring appearance, often on short notice, at a faraway place. Federal criminal process extends, often for substantial purposes, throughout the nation. But the compelled appearance in a secret grand jury room in a distant city is not always essential or justifiable. Physical presence of the witness is far from universally necessary, except perhaps where the target of the inquiry is involved. A grand jury or other agency near the witness's home may take testimony for transmittal to the panel that asserts a need for it. Other substitutes for the long trip are possible. Without precluding compelled travel in proper cases, the governing rules should require some justification, including the unsuitability of possible alternatives, for requiring a grand jury witness to testify beyond, say, one thousand miles from home (a figure that may be negotiable).

Pending bills would empower a federal court to transfer an entire investigation to a different federal district based upon judgments about such things as "the distance of the grand jury investigation from the places of residence of witnesses who have been subpoenaed, financial and other burdens placed upon the witnesses, and the existence and nature of any related investigations and court proceedings."[63] We have serious reservations about this idea, especially if, as we have suggested, the problems can be adequately managed by attending to the situations of individual witnesses directly rather than deciding that the entire investigation, the scope of which is not easily known in advance, should be bundled off to some other court and a different prosecutor's office.

ADVICE ON RIGHTS. The theoretical possession of rights is no boon to the ignorant. The witness called before the grand jury should be told of his basic rights, including the right to counsel and the privilege against

self-incrimination. He should be informed of the subject
of the inquiry and possible dangers to himself. Proposed
legislation would direct that testimony taken from a witness who was not warned of his rights could not later
be used against him, and that he could not be indicted
thereafter on account of matters to which the testimony
related. The prohibition against using testimony improperly taken seems appropriate, but the second sanction may be more severe than the competing interests
justify. More importantly, of course, it is to be hoped that
the right to advice would be respected by conscientious
prosecutors so that the question of sanctions for ignoring it would not often arise.

TRANSCRIPT OF TESTIMONY. Every grand jury witness
should be entitled to have, promptly and free of charge,
a transcript of his grand jury testimony. The supposed
interest in secrecy is no argument against this. The witness is free to record and tell his lawyer, for his own
protection, what he said to the grand jury. If he had a
perfect memory, he could have and use a perfect record.
Lacking that miraculous benefit, he faces a variety of
dangers and disadvantages. If he has meant to be truthful, he may lose opportunities to correct innocent errors.
If he means to stay truthful, he may nevertheless be led
to later contradictions by lapses of memory that could be
avoided if the transcript were available for reference. If
he must come one day to contend with the prosecutor,
his adversary will have the transcript. The embattled
witness should not be without it.

THE RECALCITRANT WITNESS. Much of the proposed
legislation seeks to assist witnesses who, for whatever
reason, choose not to cooperate with the grand jury.
Suggestions include shortening maximum terms of im-

prisonment for contempt; preventing successive punishments (that is, jailing a witness who declines to answer, recalling him when his confinement ends, then jailing him again for the renewed refusal); and allowing bail pending a contempt appeal. For the most part, the contemplated changes seem to be improvements. The existing oddity of holding a federal witness in jail for the remaining life of the grand jury seems uniquely undesirable, as does any rule that measures imprisonment by some fortuitous irrelevancy.

IMMUNITY. Several bills would return to the rule of "transactional" rather than "use" immunity. How one responds to this issue depends very much on visceral qualities and relatively little on empirical data, because relevant facts seem to be notably absent. The issue sounds simple enough: it pits the interest in truth against the danger of self-incrimination. Libertarians side generally with the broader immunity, fearing that use immunity will in fact allow undetected transgressions against the privilege. Our own judgment on this issue is that the libertarian case, however appealing rhetorically, has not been made. The stance of the Supreme Court majority has given us several years of experience with the narrower, testimonial immunity. If this has produced the evils feared by the dissenters, they remain to be persuasively detected and documented. Until or unless that job can be done, we think the interest in discovering the truth should continue to be served.

It is important, albeit difficult, to define this problem with care. Proponents of the broadest definition of the privilege against self-incrimination are often concerned with the morbid uses of grand juries (and other investigative agencies) to pry into political beliefs and associations, matters of conscience, and other domains that ought generally to be inviolable. Realistically, however, the desired protections are not achieved by wide definitions of "immunity." However defined, the immunity presumably compels answers to legitimate questions. It is true that grand juries have at times pressed intrusive and unconstitutional inquiries. But those oppressions are not effectively blocked by definitions of immunity. They need to be met head-on, often by reference to constitutional protections (e.g., of free speech, association, religion, and privacy) other than the privilege against self-incrimination. Similar principles should govern legislation aimed at keeping grand juries within decent bounds. But this is a subject distinct from, and probably more important than, the scope of immunities that apply indifferently to cases of bank robbery, securities fraud, and possibly "political" crimes.

Prospective defendants. A witness subpoenaed before a New York State grand jury, unless he gives a waiver of the protection, is automatically immunized from prosecution for the things about which he testifies. The federal courts and most states, having no such rule, allow a target to be called involuntarily. Without endorsing the New York rule, we would favor a number of the proposed protections not now assured such a person.

For one, the prospective defendant, known to be such, should be advised of his situation. He should not be summoned at all if the prosecutor knows he will invoke the privilege against self-incrimination, so that the sole purpose is to have this performed before the grand jury and taken (in violation of the Constitution) as a basis for adverse inferences.

For the prospective defendant who is not called, there should be a right, in the absence of some good reason for disallowance, to appear voluntarily on request and present his version of the affair under inquiry. While we would not support a further right of a prospective defendant to call witnesses other than himself before the grand jury, his suggestions of people to be heard ought to be conveyed to, and given careful and sympathetic consideration by, the grand jurors.

Exculpatory evidence. Extending the last thought, some states require, and some reformers urge, that the prosecutor present evidence favorable to the prospective defendant. Without a more powerful demonstration than we have seen, we question the wisdom of such a general requirement. Most prosecutors have an interest in bringing only indictments on which they foresee a substantial likelihood of conviction. Toward that end, they are likely, at least very frequently, to inform the grand jury of things that seem truly and weightily exculpatory. Careful prosecutors often encourage counsel for a prospective defendant to submit evidence or legal authorities that controvert the government's position. To be sure, such a submission generally serves to alert the prosecutor to legal and factual defenses. On occasion, however, a presentation of this kind has persuaded a prosecutor to drop a case that lacked sufficient merit.

There remain difficulties in the idea of purporting to present "both sides" to a grand jury. The preliminary rehearsal of a trial in the grand jury room, but with counsel for only one side, entails dangers, or at least dubieties. Prospective defense witnesses may have their stories warped or colored unfairly in the grand jury room. It may be doubted that the average defense counsel would desire such an *ex parte* "rehearsal" of people he plans to call. Moreover, it is difficult enough as things stand to control the popular notion that a person indicted "must be guilty of something." The task is made more manageable by being able to remind trial jurors that the grand jury heard only the prosecutor's side. One may question the effects of a general understanding, however much a distortion, that the grand jury actually heard both sides.

Repetitive efforts to indict. It has been proposed that after a grand jury "has failed to return an indictment based on a transaction, set of transactions, event, or events, a grand jury inquiry into the same transactions or events shall not be initiated unless the court finds, upon a proper showing by the attorney for the Government, that the Government has discovered additional evidence relevant to such inquiry."[64] The case for this restriction does not seem to have been made.

The extent of the supposed problem leading to this proposal has not been shown in any persuasive way. While grand jury inquiries often end with indictments, they don't start out with indictments. A second grand jury may indict for crimes that look with hindsight like the very things a prior grand jury was investigating when it produced no similar indictment. But the first investigation may have gone on different premises, or premises less clear. What now seems self-evident may not have been evident at all to the earlier group, led by a prosecutor whose theories were then different or less intelligible. The test of "additional evidence" to justify the eventual indictment puts the wrong question and may lead to answers not genuinely in the public interest. That interest, as we have stressed from time to time, includes the effective prosecution of crime. It also includes the effective use of limited judicial resources. The latter need is not served by putting trial judges to work comparing grand jury transcripts to see whether a defendant could or should have been indicted sooner—or shouldn't have been indicted later because he was not indicted sooner —rather than proceeding to have the indictment tried and disposed of on its merits before a trial jury.

Unless the practice of successive efforts to indict has become far more prevalent and abusive than we perceive it to be, the provision for comparing the grand jury records is excessive, wasteful, and contrary to the public interest.

Independent ("Watergate") investigations. In the still spreading wake of Watergate, some reformers would empower a grand jury to inquire "upon its own initiative . . . into offenses against the criminal laws of the United States alleged to have been committed within [its] district by an officer or agent of the United States or any state or municipal government or by any person who, at the time of the alleged commission of the offense, was an officer or agent of the United States or of any state or municipal government."[65] A grand jury embarked upon such a self-starting investigation could have a life of a year or more, and could work with a special attorney independent of the United States attorney for the district. The idea is fraught with possibilities and dangers. It has generated a good deal of debate, much of which is responsible and interesting. It is a subject for a book of its own.

Another aspect of the same large subject is also reflected in proposed federal legislation creating an office or offices of "special prosecutor." Whatever shape the federal law takes, the idea is likely to remain open for state as well as federal experimentation. The experience around the country with special investigations and special prosecutors teaches mixed and uncertain lessons. Some such prosecutors have been splendid, fearless, fair champions of the right and effective detectors and punishers of wrongdoing. Some have been zealots whose net achievements were assaults on fundamental decencies and the rule of law. The special prosecutor, in the court-house argot, senses a need to deliver the "red meat." Having a unique and "special" assignment, often with considerable publicity, he is under heavy pressure to generate indictments and convictions. This is an obvious danger.

Recognition of the danger is a necessity, but not nec-essarily an answer to the need. Though we may wish it could always be otherwise, situations will arise that are kin to Watergate, at least in the sense that they cause the regular prosecutorial agencies to be in a position of con-flict, or seeming conflict. For example, accusations, whether well or ill founded, will be made against high executive officials, fellow members of the Cabinet in which the Attorney General sits, or the Attorney General himself. In cases of this nature, it ranges from awkward to patently unsuitable to have the Attorney General in charge of the prosecution. Assuming, then, that there will be a need from time to time, the question is as to the best means for filling it. One recommendation would be, among other things, to create a permanent office of spe-cial prosecutor but to limit the term of any given incum-bent to three years. Other safeguards against "political" taint, or its appearance, would include disqualification for this office of anyone recently high on any important campaign staff.

There are, as we have confessed, many more facets to the problem. Since they are somewhat beyond our topic as well as our expertise, we note their existence without attempting here to cope with them.

Secrecy—too much and too little. As mentioned earlier, the secrecy of grand jury proceedings serves valid ends. Like other useful ideas, however, it has been the subject both of undue extension and of frequent subversion. The overextensions include, in the federal courts and elsewhere, the withholding of grand jury transcripts from defendants on trial except that, after direct examination at trial, the grand jury testimony of a prosecution witness must be given to the defense for use in cross-examination. As a main justification for this restriction, secrecy is generally inapposite. Once a defendant is brought to trial, the reasons for secrecy are usually gone. Subject to safeguards of scope and timing—for example, to limit fabrication of evidence and tampering with witnesses— it seems desirable that grand jury transcripts be far more freely available to defendants.

The opposite problem, the violation of secrecy when it should be preserved, has also been considered earlier. Here we emphasize again that efforts to prevent or punish leaks from grand juries have been remarkably feeble. Probably the main practical obstacle to effective control has been the power and protected positions of those primarily involved with the delivery and dissemination of illicitly leaked information—the prosecutors and the media. It is difficult indeed to make the prosecutors police themselves. And the sensitive domain of the First Amendment is not an easy one in which to contrive sanctions for the dissemination of information. It should be possible, nonetheless, to grasp these nettles and protect the deep interests for which grand jury secrecy is designed without sacrificing values prized at least as much.

Adding to suggestions touched upon earlier, we note a recent bill that would make it a federal misdemeanor, punishable by a fine of up to $500 and six months in prison, to reveal grand jury activities except when disclosure is specifically allowed. Where the illicit disclosure is made to obtain money or to influence the grand jury's proceedings, the violation is punishable by as much as a $20,000 fine and five years' imprisonment.[66] These added sanctions, including the specific reaffirmation that such revelations are lawless, could certainly do no harm. But more is probably needed.

One possibility might be a statutory provision for substantial money recoveries, without necessary proof of technical "actual damages," in favor of those affected by disclosure of grand jury secrets. An exception could be made for leaks later found to be justified in the interests of ferreting out corruption or other forms of official misconduct. The threat of liability, even as thus qualified, might deter members of prosecution staffs who now find it agreeable to leak information with effective impunity. As things stand now, there is no question that people inside the courthouse are frequently responsible for deliberate, often malicious, always lawless breaches of the grand jury secrecy they are enjoined to help enforce.

It has been suggested that the media themselves should be exposed to liability for deliberately disseminating information unlawfully passed through the wall of secrecy that is supposed to surround the grand jury. The suggestion has some initial appeal. Grand jury leaks, as a practical matter, occur and are injurious mainly because they are broadcast in the press and other media. There is rarely even a pretense that these breaches serve any public end beyond the premise that anything a journalist can find out must be published. And it seems clear by now that the public's "right to know," along with the right to tell, has limits that may be passed when other vital interests are at stake.

Nevertheless, we would not favor, without an exceedingly compelling demonstration of need—a demonstration that has not yet been made—a provision for liability upon the media. The underlying concern in this view is, of course, for the freedom of speech and press guaranteed by the First Amendment. We do not pretend to decide whether a narrow provision for damages for publishing grand jury leaks would necessarily be held unconstitutional in the courts. The question is probably open in the sense that confident predictions of what the Supreme Court might do are not possible. It is clear enough "that the press is not free to publish with impunity everything and anything it desires to publish."[67] It may be mulcted for libel, for intentional fraud, and for other abuses. It is equally clear, however, to put the matter broadly and tersely, that restrictions on free expression in the media and elsewhere are disfavored in the law until it is shown that other, less painful measures are insufficient to fill some vital need.

At least as of now, we would, as a matter of policy, however the Supreme Court might rule, reject the idea of sanctions against the media for telling grand jury secrets. Whenever a new species of liability becomes available against the organs of communication, there is an inhibition upon free expression, or a threatened inhibition, since litigation is itself a burdensome and costly business. It has not been shown thus far that the evil of grand jury leaks is so great, or that alternative cures are so plainly ineffectual, as to warrant our hobbling the media with damage suits. Future experience may come to justify such dangerous experiments. For now it seems sufficient that journalists can probably be forced in proper cases to reveal (to grand juries among other inquirers) the sources of their leaked information. By this and other means, aggrieved people could reach the offenders with the kind of damage suit we have suggested.

Grand jury reports. We would not forbid grand jury reports, but would provide limits upon their subject matter and some judicial supervision over their issuance. A New York statute enacted in 1964 provides what may be a useful model. It allows grand jury reports:

(a) Concerning misconduct, non-feasance or neglect in public office by a public servant as the basis for a recommendation of removal or disciplinary action; or

(b) Stating that after investigation of a public servant it finds no misconduct, non-feasance or neglect in office by him provided that such public servant has requested the submission of such report; or

(c) Proposing recommendations for legislative, executive or administrative action in the public interest based upon stated findings.

The statute goes on to require submission of the report to a judge, who may make an order "accepting and filing such report as a public record" only if satisfied that it is based upon sufficient evidence, that it is the kind of report allowed by the above-quoted criteria, and that the persons named were given a chance to appear before the grand jury. Even then, the report must be sealed for at least thirty-one days after it is served on every public official it names, to allow any such official to file an answer or take an appeal or both. There are additional restrictions and protective arrangements too detailed for description here.

A similar federal statute, applying to special grand juries, is part of the Organized Crime Control Act of 1970. It provides safeguards similar to those in the New York enactment, and the special grand jury's reporting function is limited to situations involving "organized criminal activity."

Without stopping to exhaust every detail, we think these statutes represent a wise compromise between having grand juries pronounce without limit upon the work of public servants and forbidding such scrutiny altogether.[68]

Publicity and fanfare. We reiterate the suggestion that press conferences and other celebrations to mark the issuance of indictments are no proper business of prosecutors. The singling out of particular defendants in this fashion—whether or not it is thought to further any end beyond glorifying the prosecutor—has no legitimate use. The indictment of celebrities presents difficulties enough without this gratuitous enhancement. Surely, there is no ground to fear that the grand jury's charge against someone already notable or notorious will escape the notice of the media. Indictments are public documents, routinely scrutinized by reporters.

This is not to question the propriety of the prosecutor's supplying full information and answering journalists' questions about technical or other professional questions. It is only to say that the special dramatization of an indictment by press conference, on TV or otherwise, can do no good, only harm.

The list of proposed safeguards—of checks and balances—to modulate the powers of prosecutors and grand juries is in a sound American tradition. The federal Constitution, in which the grand jury has had its secure place for all of our national history, was written in substantial measure on the premise that power must always be balanced to the extent possible, that the corrupting influence of absolute power must be avoided at all costs, that we must build our government with an awareness that human beings are after all not angels. That kind of pragmatic wisdom should continue to guide us. It should be applied to the grand jury as well as to our other fundamental institutions of government.

At the same time, we must know in a complex world that power must be lodged somewhere and that people inevitably make a difference. Prosecutors bent on self-aggrandizement or fired with too much certainty can subvert the most elaborate safeguards. We must work steadily to improve the caliber of our prosecutors—probably to depoliticize the office and to reconsider the almost unfettered discretion these officials now enjoy. The general problem of selecting, and better regulating, prosecutors plainly transcends, though it directly affects, the subject of the present book. But such matters are separable only in the sense that finite amounts of reading and writing are about all we can manage in any allotted time period. The interconnections are worth mentioning, if only not to lose sight of them.

The most important link of all is the one between the grand jury and the citizen who both staffs it and is touched by it. The safeguard of paramount value, for the grand jury as for other agencies of a democratic society, is the steady concern and attention of the people. One of our greatest judges, Learned Hand, put the thought with characteristic splendor when he said:

> Liberty lies in the hearts of men and women; when it dies there, no constitution, no law, no court can save it; no constitution, no law, no court can even do much to help it. While it lies there it needs no constitution, no law, no court to save it.[69]

The high hopes of the Founders when they preserved the grand jury are for all of us to save if we know enough and care enough.

Notes
and Index

Notes

1. *United States v. Calandra,* 414 U.S. 338, 343 (1974).
2. Melville Bigelow, *History of Procedure in England,* 325–26 (1880).
3. *The New York Times v. Sullivan,* 376 U.S. 254, 276 (1964).
4. *In re Horowitz,* 482 F.2d 72, 80 (2d Cir.), *cert. denied,* 414 U.S. 867 (1973).
5. *Petition of Borden Co.,* 75 F. Supp. 857 (N.D. Ill. 1948).
6. *In re Miller,* 17 Fed. Cas. 295 (No. 9,552) (C.C.D. Ind. 1878).
7. *United States v. Procter & Gamble Co.,* 356 U.S. 677, 681 n.6 (1958).
8. *United States v. Estepa,* 471 F.2d 1132 (2d Cir. 1972).
9. *United States v. Calandra, supra,* 414 U.S. at 349–50.
10. *United States v. Mackey,* 405 F. Supp. 854, 867 (E.D.N.Y. 1975).
11. *Cobbs v. Robinson,* 528 F.2d 1331, 1338 (2d Cir. 1975), *cert. denied,* 96 S.Ct 1419 (1976).
12. *Taylor v. Louisiana,* 419 U.S. 522 (1975).
13. *Pierre v. Louisiana,* 306 U.S. 354 (1939).
14. *Smith v. Texas,* 311 U.S. 128, 132 (1940).
15. *Peters v. Kiff,* 407 U.S. 493, 503–4 (1972).
16. *Taylor v. Louisiana, supra,* 419 U.S. at 530.
17. *Id.* at 541–42.
18. *Carter v. Jury Commission of Greene County,* 396 U.S. 320 (1970).
19. In re the Matter of Four Reports of the Nassau County Grand Jury Designated as Panel No. 4 for the April 1975 Term of the County Court of Nassau County (Nassau Cty. Ct. April 27, 1976).
20. *United States v. Remington,* 208 F.2d 567, 573 (2d Cir. 1953), *cert. denied,* 347 U.S. 913 (1954).
21. *In re Groban,* 352 U.S. 330, 352–53 (1957) (Black, J., dissenting).

22. *Talley v. California*, 362 U.S. 60, 64 (1960).
23. *N.A.A.C.P. v. Alabama*, 357 U.S. 449, 462 (1958).
24. *Bursey v. United States*, 466 F.2d 1059, 1089 (9th Cir. 1972).
25. *United States v. Briggs*, 514 F.2d 794, 806 (5th Cir. 1975).
26. Quoted in Victor Navasky, *Kennedy Justice*, 396 (1971).
27. *United States v. Mandujano*, 425 U.S. 564, 581 (1976).
28. Samuel Dash, *The Indicting Grand Jury: A Critical Stage*, 10 Amer. Crim. L. Rev. 807 (1972).
29. "The Grand Jury System Defended," *New York Law Journal*, January 22, 1976, pp. 1, 4.
30. *United States v. Morse*, 292 Fed. 273, 278–79 (S.D.N.Y. 1922).
31. *Brady v. Maryland*, 373 U.S. 83 (1963).
32. *United States v. Mandujano, supra*, 425 U.S. at 573–75.
33. *Id.* at 598–600.
34. *Kastigar v. United States*, 406 U.S. 441, 446 (1972).
35. *Id.* at 449.
36. *Id.* at 453.
37. *The Compulsory Process Clause*, 75 Mich. L. Rev. 71, 170 (1974).
38. *Earl v. United States*, 361 F.2d 531, 534 (D.C. Cir. 1966).
39. *Id.* at 534 n.l.
40. Quoted in Henry Bull, *Nürnberg Trial*, 7 F.R.D. 175, 178 (1947).
41. 8 J. Wigmore, *Evidence*, §2362 at 736 (McNaughton Rev. 1961).
42. Cal. Ann. Penal Code §939.91 (Supp. 1976)
43. *The Grand Jury "Presentment": Foul Blow or Fair Play?*, 55 Col. L. Rev. 1103, 1136 (1955).
44. *People v. McCabe*, 266 N.Y.S. 363, 367 (Sup. Ct. Queens Co. 1933).
45. *Matter of Woods v. Hughes*, 9 N.Y. 2d 144, 155 (1961).
46. *Application of United Electrical, Radio & Machine Workers*, 111 F. Supp. 858 (S.D.N.Y. 1953).
47. *United States v. Briggs, supra*, 514 F.2d at 794, 804, 806.
48. *Id.* at 805.
49. Reply Brief for the United States in *United States v. Nixon*, page 20.
50. Helene Schwartz, *Demythologizing the Historic Role of the Grand Jury*, 10 Amer. Crim. L. Rev. 701, 761 (1972).
51. *Wood v. Georgia*, 370 U.S. 375, 390 (1962).
52. *Eliminate the Grand Jury*, 64 J. Crim. Law and Criminology 174 (1973).
53. *United States v. Mandujano, supra*, 425 U.S. at 576.
54. *Carroll v. United States*, 16 F. 2d 951, 953 (2d Cir.), *cert. denied*, 273 U.S. 763 (1927).
55. *Id.* at 953.
56. *Id.* at 953–54.
57. *Brown v. United States*, 245 F. 2d 549, 555 (8th Cir. 1957).
58. *Ponzi v. Fessenden*, 285 U.S. 254, 262 (1922).

59. *Springer v. Philippine Islands,* 277 U.S. 189, 201–2 (1928).
60. The case name, because it was in partial form an appeal directed against the district judge, is *United States v. Cox,* 342 F. 2d 167 (5th Cir.), *cert. denied,* 381 U.S. 935 (1965).
61. *United States v. Cowan,* 524 F. 2d 504, 513 (5th Cir. 1975).
62. H.R. 11660, 94th Cong., 2d Sess. §3328 (1976).
63. H.R. 94, 95th Cong., 1st Sess. §3330B(f) (2) (1977). See also S.3274, 94th Cong., 2d Sess. §3330A(g) (1976); H.R. 11660, 94th Cong., 2d Sess. §3330A(g) 1976).
64. S. 3274, 94th Cong., 2d Sess. §3330A(h) (1976); H.R. 11660, 94th Cong., 2d Sess. §3330A(h) (1976). See also H.R. 94, 95th Cong., 1st Sess. §3329(e) (1977).
65. S.3274, 94th Cong., 2d Sess. §3330(a) (1) (1976); H.R. 11660, 94th Cong., 2d Sess. §3330(a) (1) (1976). See also H.R. 94, 95th Cong., 1st Sess. §3330(a) (1) (1977).
66. H.R. 94, 95th Cong., 1st Sess. §1512 (1977).
67. *Branzburg v. Hayes,* 408 U.S. 665, 683 (1972).
68. The New York statute is §190.85 of that state's Criminal Procedure Law. We are indebted to Richard H. Kuh, Esq., former District Attorney of New York County, for calling its omission to our attention in a letter concerning the earlier version of this work in *The New Leader.* The federal statute is 18 United States Code §3333.
69. Learned Hand, *The Spirit of Liberty,* 190 (1952).

Index

Note: Throughout, the words "of grand jury" are implied for most entries as, for example, "selection (of grand jury)." See also grand jury entry.